CREATING MINIATURE FOOD

FOR DOLLS' HOUSES

Emma Ferdinando

CREATING MINIATURE FOOD

FOR DOLLS' HOUSES

THE CROWOOD PRESS

Contents

. . . .

CHAPTER 1

Introduction

. . . .

have always been fascinated by scale – by things that are too big or too small. A fly's eye under a microscope, or a whale hanging from the roof of a museum were always the inspiration for me. Some of my work used to be painting huge murals for advertising and in people's homes, but I turned instead to the more convenient creation of pieces for dolls' houses and have done this now for more than twenty years. Trying to make each piece as realistic as possible can become quite an obsession and I know that thousands of people find the challenge to be an enjoyable and absorbing pastime.

Creating miniature worlds for dolls' houses involves a lot of different skills, but making food is a great way to start. Tiny food can be quite forgiving as a project because no two real foodstuffs are ever identical and the sizes and colours can vary endlessly. The pieces I am creating in this book are predominantly made using polymer clay. This type of clay is easily available, cheap and comes in an amazing range of colours. Most of the other resources I use are also basic and easily available. I began learning to make tiny food before

the internet was around, so I had to source most products from shops and develop a lot of methods for myself. Nowadays, social media can provide a huge source of ideas and alternative methods; a quick scroll can give you so much inspiration.

This book will also introduce you to some basic model-making techniques, such as caning, dry-brushing, mould-making and so on, which can be used in lots of ways to make all kinds of different dolls' house food and accessories. You are limited only by your imagination!

INSPIRATION

Depending on what kind of projects you have done in the past, getting started can be tricky. A good idea is to choose one thing rather than a whole meal and take your time with it. The advantage of making pieces using clay is that if you're not happy, just squish it up and start again. If you have, or are planning, a dolls' house, this will provide a good source of inspiration – for example, what style or

◀ Getting settled with a cup of coffee and a snack ready to dream up your first miniature project.

Using a real apple on a plate to work out what size your model apple should be compared to its plate.

show you the little touches of colour or texture that make a piece 'real'. Besides, copying something from life makes the final piece completely unique and truly yours.

SCALE

Getting the scale right is something people really worry about when making dolls' house pieces. However, once you have made one or two things, you will usually start to get a feel for scale and it becomes much more natural and easy to judge. The usual scale sizes are 1/6, which means 1 inch for every 6 inches in real life. This scale is used for Barbie, Sindy, Action Man and G.I. Joe and dolls of that size.

The next is 1/12, which means 1 inch for every 12 inches in real life. This scale is the most usual in modern dolls' houses and the one I will mostly be using in this book. Old dolls' houses, such as the one my mother had in the 1940s, were 1/16. This size is slightly smaller than the modern 1/12, but a lot of things can be compatible for both, for instance a 1/12 side plate is a perfect size for a 1/16 dinner plate. Everything just looks a little more dainty in 1/16. If you are working on a 1/16 house, you may have to do a lot more measuring than with 1/12, but once you know the measurements you need for plates and so on, lots of online stores will sell these by measurement rather than scale.

The next scale down is 1/24, which is half the size of 1/12 and is often the size used when you buy kits to make an entire room, a shop and so on. You need good eyes to make pieces this small, but if using the caning method it is relatively easy to keep shrinking the piece until it fits this size. It is a good idea to keep detail to a minimum, as lots of fussy detail at this scale will only be a blur. After this, the scales go down to 1/48 and on into the hundreds, which are used in dioramas and railway

period is the house and what would the people in it have around the house? A fancy Victorian house would have a beautiful fruit display and fresh produce in the kitchen, raw meat, vegetables and crusty bread. A modern-style apartment might have pizza or sushi on the table.

Another good place to look for ideas is cookbooks and food magazines. I always pick up the latest free food magazine in the supermarket. The photos of food are usually clear and close up, which helps when understanding how to create the look of real food. As tempting as it is, copying other miniaturist pieces, or assuming that you know what a cabbage looks like, are not always successful: working from life or from photos of real food is really important. Copying other models of food means that you may end up accentuating any mistakes the model-maker has made and potentially missing something that gives the piece a sense of realism. Following a reference will models. Food at this point becomes something better represented by using textured paints, rather than trying to model it individually.

I have found that the more you work in one particular scale, the more you get used to what size things should be and it becomes something that you can just do by eye. Of course, you can measure the sizes exactly if you wish – for example, for 1/12 scale, measure the real item then divide this by 12 to achieve the desired scale. I find the easiest way is to have objects around you of the correct scale to compare your pieces to. Looking at an apple on a plate or in your hand, for example, you can see what size that apple should be in comparison. It is therefore a good idea to buy some plates, serving dishes and jars in the scale of your choice and keep them near whilst making your pieces so that you can keep an eye on the size.

Sometimes if things have layers and additional pieces, they can become oversized. I find that cakes tend to expand with each layer of icing. A cake that gets out of control and too wide for its plate can be cut smaller with a cutter and re-iced. The good thing about starting with food for your dolls' house is that food is a very forgiving subject. It is always a bit wobbly and irregular – an apple can be as small as the palm of your hand, or as large as two hands, depending on the look you want.

Battenburg cakes large and small. The full-size cake is 12cm tall and its 1/12 dolls' house version is 1cm tall. These cakes come in snack sizes, too.

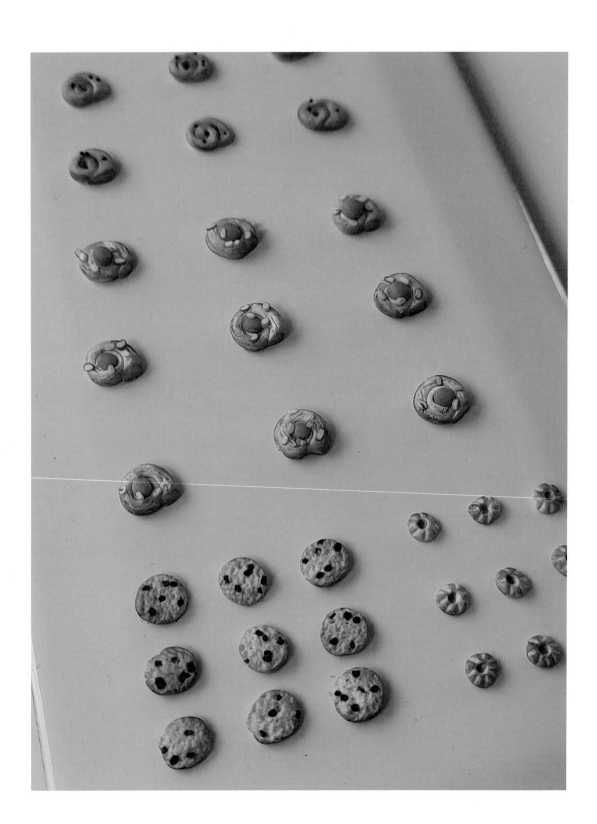

CHAPTER 2

Getting Started

. . . .

efore beginning your miniature projects, it is a good idea to create a quiet workspace, where your pieces won't be knocked or squashed. A good light is important for working on a small scale; craft lamps are great, although a desk lamp with a daylight bulb would also work. Your work surface needs to be flat and protected from razor cuts with a cutting board or thick mounting board. I use a fresh sheet of white paper on top of the board for each new project, as I find it easier to judge colour and texture against a white background. Paper is also good because the pieces don't stick to it too much, making it easier to move them on to a tile for baking. Some people like to work on an acetate sheet because the clay piece sticks enough that you can pick up the sheet and see the model from all angles without it falling off.

BAKING

I recommend using a white tile on which to bake your items. If a piece is delicate or likely to break, it is best modelled directly on the tile, thereby avoiding the risk of breakage when transferring from the work surface. The polymer clay, once baked on the tile, comes off quite easily and stray colour can be wiped off before starting your next make.

White ceramic tiles can be bought easily from hardware or tile shops and are the best thing to bake your pieces on as they conduct heat well and the objects don't stick to them. I find using a metal tray sometimes increases the temperature too much for the clay and can cause it to burn. Modelling a piece directly on the tile means you don't have to move it around while it is still soft, and cutting pieces on tile is also better as the surface does not scratch.

MAGNIFICATION

People often ask whether I use magnification whilst I'm working. I think that this is a personal preference, but other than my usual glasses I don't find it helps; it just seems to make my fingers seem huge

◀ Lots of tiny pastries and biscuits on a ceramic tile waiting to be put in the oven.

and ungainly. Craft lamps, however, often have a built-in magnifying glass if you decide to use one.

STORAGE AND SCALE

It is a good idea to arrange the things you will need around you so that they are within easy reach. You will need pots for tools and a set of little drawers, such as those used to store nails and screws is also helpful. You will also need a few plastic bags in which to store baked and unbaked pieces (separately). Unbaked polymer clay cannot be stored in hard plastic boxes or storage drawers as it reacts with the plastic and melts it; similarly, it can't come into contact with baked clay as it has the same effect. A few mixing pots and lolly sticks are also handy. In this book, I have used clear plastic disposable shot glasses to mix liquid clay, texture gel and resin. I have done this only so that it is easier to see the mixture in photographs. In reality, I use a mixture of old bottle tops, pots and paper cups, which are cheaper and not single-use plastic. Liquid clay and pigment can also be mixed on a ceramic tile and the residue wiped off afterwards.

It is also very useful when working on a project to have objects around you of the right scale, such as the plate, dish or board on which you will display the piece, or some accessories like knives or glasses so that you can judge the correct size of your item. You could even have a scale person watching over you – this is very useful when deciding how big each piece should be compared to a person. Storing projects and clay properly covered stops them from attracting dust and fluff.

CLAYS

There are many different brands of polymer clay on the market and I use a few different ones. Each type has slightly different instructions for use and different baking temperatures. It is important that you read the information on the specific clay you have chosen before baking it. These differences are why I am not giving exact temperatures for the projects, as these will vary depending on the brand of clay. The strength of pigment is also different in each type of clay, so amounts of colour are also estimated. A few experiments with mixing colour will get you used to how pigmented each clay colour is, but it is always best to use less than you think to start with, as you can always add more colour. Also, if using dry-brushed colour on your piece, the base colour should be paler so as to give a better effect with the pastel colour.

When using polymer clay, it is important to manipulate it into a good consistency for modelling. Take the clay you want to use and begin by warming it in your hands. Press and knead the clay over and over itself to make it consistently soft and pliable. Adding colour involves taking small amounts of coloured clay and kneading and

The colours of polymer clay I have used most, along with a couple of standard mixes.

folding this into the base colour until it is a solid colour. This mixing is particularly important with translucent clay, because if not thoroughly blended the baked piece will contain streaks of translucent colour. If you mix too much clay, leftovers can be stored in a plastic bag for another project.

The other type of clay that I refer to is liquid clay. This is just translucent polymer clay but in a liquid form. It can be used to seal pieces, as well as to glue them together, or glue them to plates and so on. It is also used to make sauces and icing, and can be coloured with acrylic paint or pastels when a more translucent look is required. Another use for liquid clay is to mix it with regular clay to form thick pastes and spreads such as peanut butter or chocolate icing. I prefer to use liquid clay as glue as often as I can in projects. It can be used on baked clay objects that can then be re-baked to set the liquid clay.

This is a list of my most often used clay colours:

* translucent – my most used 'colour', as when mixed with other clays it gives them a natural juicy quality and also helps to make them more flexible; translucent clay is white until baked
* white – can be a little crumbly, so I often mix it with a small amount of translucent clay to give it some strength and flexibility
* caramel brown
* dark brown
* golden yellow
* basic red
* burgundy red (useful for fruits and berries, as well as for meat)
* olive green
* leaf green
* black.

I also use the following colours, some of which can be made by mixing with other colours, or by tinting with pastel pigments:

* light lemon yellow
* orange
* blue
* purple
* candy pink
* aqua blue (only used in the Liquorice Allsorts project)
* silver (can be used when making fish and also marble boards, but is not essential).

With these colours it is possible to make all the colour mixes that you will need for your tiny food projects. Following are three standard mixes that will help to speed things along:

Meat mix (raw)

This mix consists of translucent clay mixed with tiny amounts of white, burgundy red and dark brown. Looking at an image of the meat you are creating, start by adding a tiny amount of each colour to the translucent clay, then adjust as necessary according to the type of meat it is.

Meat mix (cooked)

This mix will begin with white clay and then tiny amounts of burgundy red, dark brown and caramel brown. Again, the amount of each colour will vary depending on the type of meat. Some meats, like bacon or ham, may look more real with a couple of slightly different colour mixes in one piece.

Pastry mix

This mix is for anything baked, such as bread, pies, biscuits and so on. The mix consists of white clay with a tiny amount of golden yellow and caramel brown. For bread, very little colour is required, as most of the colour comes from the dry-brushed colour effect, but for biscuits and pie crust it would be a little darker.

Using a soft dry brush and artists' pastels to add layers of gradual colour to the clay before baking to give it a natural look.

Layering sheets of different coloured clay on top of one another and pressing them together creates either an ombré or a striped effect.

TECHNIQUES

Layering

Layering is a method used to create a striped appearance in the clay. Coloured sheets of clay are layered on top of each other, then pressed down to make the stripes as thin as required. This method is used with different shades of green to make the layers in corncob leaves and the stripes of a prawn's body. It is also used to create a fade-in colour such as when making lettuce, where you start by layering a dark colour and then increasingly paler colours on top, so that when pressed together the colour fades from one side of the clay to the other.

Chopping

This method is used to create an appearance of mixed ingredients, such as the inside of a fruit cake or a salami sausage. It is done by taking pieces of the chosen colours and chopping them up

Chopping different coloured clays together using the single-sided razor creates a textural multicoloured look that is good for projects like fruit cake.

together with a single-sided razor blade (*see below* for the tools required for these projects). After you have chopped the pieces, re-form them and chop again. The more times you do this, the finer the mix of colours in the final piece. It can also produce a good effect for granite or corkboards.

Caning

Caning is a well-used technique in the making of miniatures, but it does take a bit of practice to get used to. I would suggest starting with a simple design such as a bull's eye or a biscuit. Begin by creating a disc of colours using a baton of the central colour, then wrap this in an even ribbon of the next colour, then the next, so as to create a fat disc with the layers of colour in the middle.

Next, the cane needs to be made smaller in width, but much longer. Take the disc in your thumb and forefinger and wrap them as much around the disc as you can. Begin to push your finger and thumb together, pushing the disc evenly around the edge. The disc should begin to reduce in width and start to be a little longer. Turn the disc while squeezing in order to keep the pressure even. As soon as the disc starts to get longer, you can gently draw your hand down the length of the cane, pulling it longer. It is very tempting just to roll the baton on your work surface to lengthen it, but this can cause the pattern inside to become twisted.

As the cane gets longer, it can be cut into manageable pieces, which can then be pulled separately. Only once the canes are as required can you give them a quick roll on the work surface to make sure that the outside of the cane is nice and smooth and round. Some parts of the cane, the ends in particular, will not retain the design very well and that is to be expected. Once the cane has been pulled completely, cut off the fatter and less perfect ends.

Caning is the method by which you can create an effect within a disc of clay, then pull and shrink it to make it smaller while keeping the integrity of the image inside. Perfect for a project such as fruit slices.

Canes of clay can be baked and sliced, or left unsliced for texturing and shaping later. If you choose to store your cane unbaked, wrap it in a plastic bag, then when you come to use it hold it in your hand to warm up for a few minutes to avoid it being crumbly when cut. The caning technique, once mastered, can be used for any project where lots of similar objects have to be made, such as sweets and fruit slices, or even book pages or butterfly wings.

Moulding

In this book I often use silicone moulds to create pieces. To make these moulds, I use a two-part silicone moulding medium that is easily available in craft stores. To make the moulds or to capture textures to use in your pieces, mix equal parts of the moulding medium and knead them together

Using a two-part mould-making medium, you can make moulds of any small object or texture.

CLAY PROBLEMS

Too soft or sticky clay

Polymer clay becomes softer and stickier as it gets warm which is helpful for modelling, but if it becomes too soft putting your piece in the fridge for a little while will firm it up. Some clays are softer than others and hot hands don't help.

Over- or under-baked clay

It is important to follow the instructions for baking on your chosen make of clay, as they do vary. Under-baked clay is very brittle and crumbly, but this is not a problem as it just needs to bake in the oven a little longer. Overbaked clay, however, is not salvageable. Overbaked clay can be cracked or discoloured or literally burnt. This happens not because of the amount of time a piece is in the oven, but because the temperature is too hot.

One reason this can happen unexpectedly is if you bake your pieces on a metal tray, or wrapped around a piece of wire. Metal continues to heat up as you cook and so makes the clay hotter than it should be. This is the reason I like to work on a tile (*see above*). When working with wire, I would suggest checking the piece often and taking it out a little earlier than the stated cooking time. Well-baked clay feels firm and elastic to the touch and if you push it with a stick, it bounces back.

the same way that you would mix clay. Any small object such as a seed pod, bead or leaf can then be pressed into the mould mix and left for the mix to set before removing. These moulds can be used as they are, or clay can be baked in them. To mould the clay, make sure that it is nicely warmed in your hand and pliable, form it into a ball and push it carefully into the mould, ensuring that no air gets in with it. Once it is well pressed into the mould, place it in the fridge for a few minutes to firm up before taking it out of the mould. Using a cocktail stick to help lever the clay out is fine, as you can tidy the base afterwards.

Once released from the mould, you can add colour to the piece. It is also possible to bake the clay in the silicone mould if dry-brush colouring is not required. Using a mould with liquid clay creates really fine detail. It is fine to bake moulded items more than once if you need to use liquid clay to stick them together, or add extra pieces to a project.

Storage problems

Baked and unbaked clay must not be stored together as they react with each other, causing both to become melted and sticky. The same reaction occurs when you store unbaked clay in hard plastic such as boxes or drawers. Soft plastic bags are the best way to store both types of clay.

Storing uncooked canes and pieces of clay in plastic bags keeps them clean and separate, ready to use for later projects.

It is also not a good idea to store or display items on a windowsill or in strong sunlight, as some colours can fade in the clay. If unbaked clay has been stored for a while it becomes quite crumbly, but this can be remedied by warming it in your hand for a while before trying to cut it.

Fluff

Fluff and dust are an issue when working with clay on a small scale. However much you wash your hands and keep your space clean, fluff still gets on your unbaked clay, especially the pale colours. Some miniaturists wear plastic gloves when working, which can help. Make sure that the towel you use for your hands is white and avoid wearing colourful fluffy jumpers when modelling. It is possible before baking to scrape off fluff with a razor, but quite often I find a lot of it melts off in the baking process, or is brushed off when applying dry-brushed colour.

Fine sandpaper can also be used to rub off embedded fluff after a project has been baked.

TOOLS

The various tools I use for the projects in this book have been gathered over years of making dolls' house items. They are all easy to get hold of and none of them is technical. The single-sided razor blade is the most important tool for working in polymer clay – a knife blade is too wide and blunt to make clean cuts. I bought my single-sided razor blade in a kitchen shop, but they are also available from chemists and online craft shops. The razor is, of course, very sharp and must be handled with care. Always slice away from your hands and leave the razor in a place where it can be seen, as most of the times I've cut myself have been by leaning on or brushing against the razor accidentally

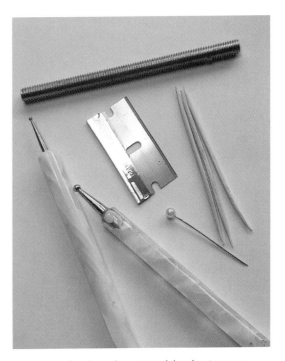

A selection of tools used to cut, model and texture your miniature food projects.

when it has not been stored away correctly. When using the razor to cut baked clay, it is best to cut it while still warm and slightly soft from the oven. If the idea of cutting baked clay worries you, an alternative is to chill unbaked clay in the fridge and then cut it. You can then bake the clay after cutting. This will also ensure that you get a clean cut without squashing the piece you have made.

Other tools that will be needed are:

* ball-ended tools, which are used in icing and nail art as well as crafts; they come in packs of different sizes
* cocktail sticks
* pins/needles
* small rolling pin; acrylic ones are available from icing shops, although you can use any small tube-shaped object like a piece of pipe or the handle of a tool
* cutters, lids or drinking straws in different widths that you can use to cut pastry shapes and cookies
* fine-ended craft tweezers
* wire
* fine sandpaper for sanding down the edges of projects like marble slabs
* icing nozzles, for icing and cutting shapes
* lolly sticks or plant sticks for mixing.

For the peacock feather project, you may also need permanent markers, nail scissors and white feathers from the craft shop or collected outside.

OTHER MATERIALS

Other materials I have used in the projects are:

Varnish

I use a varnish specifically created for polymer clay, which may react with other types of varnishes. Some people use nail varnish to seal items, but after a few months this will react and degrade the clay. There are different finishes of varnish – gloss, satin and matt. Baked clay doesn't always need varnishing, for example if a dull finish is required. I tend to use mainly gloss varnish; for a semi-gloss finish, or to bring out texture, I apply the varnish then dab it off to reinstate the texture.

Glue

This is a constant source of debate among miniaturists, as there are so many types of glue and they vary greatly. Gel-type superglue would seem to be the obvious choice, but it has its problems. I do use this if I have to apply a really tiny part to a piece, but otherwise I try to avoid it as it can become crumbly over time and if not totally dry reacts with varnish. Mostly, I use liquid clay to hold pieces together or attach items to plates and bowls. If it is an item that can't be baked, however, such as a wooden board with pieces on it, it is best to use a clear glue made for use with craft plastics.

Resin

This is used to create the illusion of water or a wet surface. It comes in a pack with two liquids that you mix and allow to dry. It is great for drinks, jellies and jams. It can also be used on finished pieces as a thick varnish.

Texture gel

I use this to create thick pastes and icing. It is used ordinarily to add to artists' acrylic paint to create a thick texture. It can be spread or piped on to a baked piece, but cannot be put in the oven. It is available from art supply stores.

Accent beads

These are tiny decorative balls used in nail art as well as craft; they are sometimes called 'bead caviar'. They are not essential as you can make tiny beads using clay, but I find them to be very handy.

Scenic sprinkle

This is used in model- and diorama-making and usually represents grass, mud or gravel. I use it to represent cut herbs or spices on miniature pieces. If you don't wish to buy a bag of sprinkle, it is possible to make it by colouring pencil shavings with paint, letting them dry and scrunching them up. Brown sprinkle well ground up makes good soil, which can be added to projects like potatoes, carrots and other root vegetables.

Model-makers' foam

This is usually green plastic foam that is used by model-makers to make trees and bushes in railway sets and dioramas. It can be really useful as a decoration for finished pieces, as it creates the look of a garnish of herbs or salad leaves.

Talcum powder

This is useful for a project that needs to look floury or powdery, such as the top of baked bread, jelly babies or Turkish delight. Some model-makers also use cornstarch for this. It also stops clay sticking to your fingers.

Silica sand

This clear sand can be useful to give the look of sugar, ice or salt in a project and can be bought at an aquarium shop.

Button thread

This thread is thicker than average thread, but is more flexible and paintable than wire. It is good to use as stalks when making fruit and vegetables. It can be attached with liquid clay and baked in the oven.

Dishes and plates

Having dishes and plates of your chosen scale around while working is really helpful for judging scale. They are also great to serve and display your mini food on. Whilst it is quite possible to make plates and dishes, I like the different texture that using china or metal plates brings to a piece. When choosing plates and dishes, think about the style and era of your dolls' house so that the crockery fits into the aesthetic of the rooms. Lots of online companies sell crockery of all styles, ranging from very fine white bone china to rough earthenware or even silver.

Finding which kinds of plates and dishes work best with the style, age and size of your dolls' house. These will help you to keep the scale of your food projects looking correct.

TEXTURING

I am always on the lookout around the house and outside for textured bits and bobs, from which I can take mould impressions to use on miniatures. Creating a good lifelike texture on a piece is really important if you want a realistic feel. It also allows the dry-brushed colour to accentuate the features of the food. Here are some things that I use to texture pieces:

* sandpaper – great for bread, cakes, biscuits and chicken skin
* scrunched-up tin foil – useful for soft cheese rinds and the texture of a steak

Adding texture to your projects gives them a realistic feel and can be done with a toothbrush, sandpaper, a toothpick or a textured mould.

* toothbrush – makes a fine and random texture for baked goods
* fine netting fabric – creates scales on fish skin
* a bolt – in the celery project I used a bolt to create stripes in the celery skin
* silicone imprints – extremely useful for adding texture to leaves and vegetables. They are made the same way as the moulds, using silicone moulding medium.

COLOURING YOUR PIECES

Adding colour using a dry- or wet-brush technique gives your food a realistic feel. You will need a basic set of artists' soft chalk pastels, as well as some brushes – one medium-sized soft brush, one very fine pointed soft brush and a flat, thin soft brush. To add blushes of colour to your pieces, just brush over the dry pastel stick and sweep the colour gently on to unbaked clay. Start with just a little, as you can build up the colour. For more defined darker areas like the stripes on a fish's skin, wet the fine pointed brush and create a sort of watercolour mix with the chalk pastel. You can also use the chalk to colour resin, liquid clay and texture gel. For a really white colour, though, it is better to use an acrylic paint in the mix.

A new set of pastels may be a bit hard to get colour from initially, so use the single-sided razor to scrape off a bit of the smooth surface of the pastel to get to the powdery interior. Use this same scaping method to add the colour to liquid clays and resins. After baking, the colour is fixed, but you can add more at this point with acrylic paint. Once all the colour has been applied and the clay baked, varnish the piece to fix the paint.

A basic set of artists' pastels for colouring your pieces, with the three main brushes I used for the projects.

CHAPTER 3

Vegetable Garden

· · · · · · · · · · · · · · · · · · · ·

Vegetables are a great way to start model-ling tiny food because working from life is easy and affordable, plus vegetables are very forgiving when you are getting used to scale as they tend to come in all sorts of odd shapes and sizes. In this section we will be working a lot with moulds as they give a natural texture to the models.

I am going to start with maize and to get a good texture I have made a mould using some tiny beads lined up in neat rows pressed into the moulding medium. Tiny beads are easily available from craft shops or online.

Mix the moulding medium and carefully press in the rows of beads, keeping them close together.

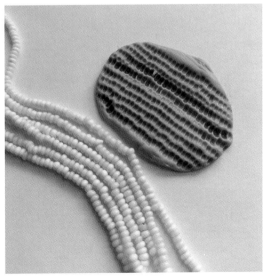

Nice straight rows create the corn kernel effect in your mould.

◀ Rather than just having your cabbage in the kitchen, they look good in the garden, too.

MAIZE

Step 1: To make the corn, mix a couple of shades of yellow with a little white and lots of translucent clay to give it a juicy look. Roll a baton-shaped piece about the length of a 1/12 dinner plate and press it into the mould. It may take a couple of

goes to get your lines of corn just where you want them. To add some different coloured kernels, use tiny balls of clay randomly placed into the mould before you press on the larger piece. If you find the clay is too soft to remove the corn easily from

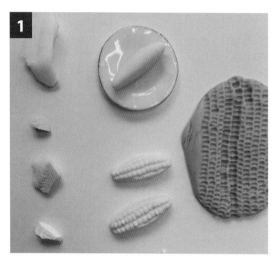

Pressing into the mould with a light yellow clay mix to create the corncobs.

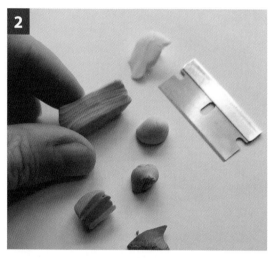

Layering different shades of green clay and pressing them down to make a thin striped effect for the corn husks.

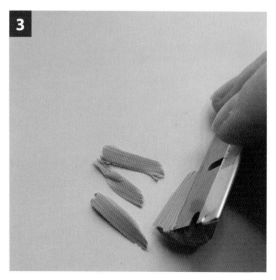

Slicing the layers very thin and at a slight angle to create the leaf shapes.

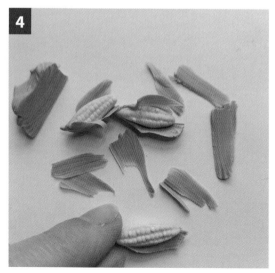

Carefully wrapping the leaves around the corncobs to create the husk.

the mould, let it firm up in the fridge for a while beforehand.

Step 2: To make the husk for the maize, mix a few shades of green, adding a little brown to some and yellow or white to others. To make the layers softer and more flexible, add some translucent clay to each one. Squash each colour flat and layer them on top of each other. Then pressing down the whole stack, cut it in half and place the cut half on top. Keep cutting and layering until you have lots of very fine stripes in your clay.

Step 3: Using your single-sided razor blade, cut some wafer-thin slices; the more ragged the edges, the better.

Step 4: Now choose the best slices and gently wrap them around the corn to create the husk. Roll the base leaves between your fingers and pull to create a stalk. Trim the stalk after you have baked the clay for a cleaner finish.

Step 5: After they have been baked and cooled, varnish just the kernels to make them look juicy and delicious.

5

There is no limit to the colours and combinations you can use to create the maize – a beautiful autumn display piece.

CABBAGE

I really enjoy making cabbages. They are very satisfying to do and the more effort you take with the dry-brushed colour, the better the result. You will need a leaf mould made from a herb with very visible veins, such as mint. Small rose or plant leaves are also fine; see what you can find when out and about. To make cabbages you need a mould that creates veins that that stick out from the leaf, rather than veins that are pressed into the leaf.

Step 1: Mix a very light spring green with translucent clay added to give the fine edges strength. Roll this clay into a baton so that you can cut

Using a mould pressed from a leaf to create cabbage leaves.

Brushing the edges of the leaves with a blush of coloured pastel.

Forming the heart of the cabbage using a cocktail stick to help.

Pressing each leaf on to the base of the cabbage and bending the leaves back for a natural look.

The finished cabbage is ready for baking after reaching the size you want and the cocktail stick has been removed.

small circles about 1cm across. Press these into the mould, trying to make the edges as thin as possible.

Step 2: Using a fine brush and some chalk pastel, push the dark green colour between the veins of the leaf, leaving the veins pale. For the outer leaves, dust the edges with a wider soft brush using a grey-blue shade.

Step 3: To build the cabbage, place a pea-sized piece of the clay on a cocktail stick.

Step 4: Wrap the first two or three leaves around the base to create the heart of the cabbage. Press the next leaves facing outwards and curled over slightly to make them appear more natural.

Step 5: Remove the stick before baking, but don't worry about cleaning up the stem until afterwards, when you can add a little more clay to the hole and re-bake.

Step 6: You can add as many leaves as required to reach the size you are looking for.

6

Cabbages after tidying the base and then baking.

CAULIFLOWER

For cauliflowers, use the same clay mix and technique as for the cabbages, just lightening the green you use to dust the leaves. You will need to make a mould from a piece of real cauliflower; cauliflowers conveniently consist of florets that get ever more miniature as they reach the centre of the plant.

Step 1: Mix a ball of white clay with a little translucent, making it slightly bigger than the pea-sized

Mixing white clay with a little translucent to give it more flexibility before putting it in your mould.

Using the leaf mould again to create the cauliflower leaves.

Making a few narrow, pointed leaves adds realism to the piece.

Adding more leaves, curling and bending them to give them a natural appearance.

ball you used for the cabbages. Place this on a cocktail stick and press it into your mould.

Step 2: Press and colour your leaves just as with the cabbages, but for cauliflower you will need a few long thin leaves as well in a paler shade of green.

Step 3: To start, wrap the thin, painted leaves over the white part of the cauliflower.

Step 4: Add the rounder leaves, pressing them close to the white part and curling them back and blending them into the stalk with a rounded modelling tool to look like they are naturally growing.

Step 5: For added realism, you can create cauliflowers in a variety of sizes.

5

Cauliflowers and cabbages of all sizes fresh from the market.

PUMPKIN AND SQUASH

It is fairly easy to model pumpkins without a mould, but making moulds for pumpkins and squash is great fun and gives good results. Decorative seed pods in all shapes and sizes used for flower arranging and potpourri are great for this. Remember to leave enough of a hole in the mould to be able get your pumpkin out easily. Of course, squash come in a whole range of colours and I particularly like the green ones, but for this project I am using a traditional pale orange mix.

Step 1: Mix a ball of light orange clay and place it on a cocktail stick. After pushing your clay into a mould, place it in the fridge as this hardens the clay and makes it easier to get out of the mould.

Step 2: Once you have removed the pumpkin from the mould, tidy up the base with a rounded tool, then use your pastels to dry-brush on some colour. To make your squash look darker and a little more Hallowe'en ready, use a darker shade down the veins and in the hole where the stalk will go.

Step 3: Roll a little clay in a paler cream colour into a baton shape and use a cocktail stick to push it into the stalk hole; spread the base slightly for a natural look. Cut the stalk after baking for a cleaner finish.

Step 4: You can also use acrylic paints to add colour after baking. Have a look at some real squash for ideas, as the range of patterns and colours is endless.

Modelling pumpkins using a variety of shapes and sizes made from natural seed pods.

Dry-brushing on pastel colour to add depth and realism.

Adding the stalk in a contrasting shade of light brown.

4

So many different shapes, colours and sizes of squash and pumpkin – the possibilities are endless. I have varnished some and left others matt.

CHAPTER 4

Pizza and Pasta

· · · · · · · · · · · · · · · · · ·

Pasta and pizza are really fun projects to work on – they are so colourful and you can use your imagination when it comes to sauces and toppings. The mixtures of whites, red and green is so evocative of the Mediterranean diet and sunshine.

In this section we are going to be using the caning technique (*see* Chapter 2) to create the items on the pasta board and some pizza toppings. The tomato cane is particularly useful for everything from salads to cheese boards and is a good thing to have in your box of ingredients.

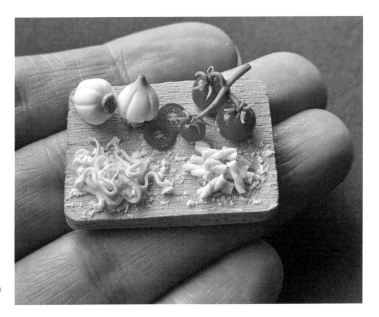

Adding a little talcum powder or cornstarch to the finished pasta gives it a floury effect.

PASTA BOARD

Making the pasta

Step 1: Mix a white clay with a tiny amount of yellow and caramel brown to make a creamy pasta colour.

Step 2: Roll this very thin using an acrylic rolling pin or the handle of one of your tools.

Step 3: For tagliatelle, cut this into thin strips and arrange into a heap. For penne pasta, roll the clay around a florists' wire, press to remove the join and bake on the wire. For fusilli, roll some of the pasta clay into two thin strings and wind them together, cutting them into lengths after baking.

1–3

From a simple pastry mix of clay you can make lots of different shapes of pasta.

Garlic bulbs

Step 1: To make the garlic, mix white clay with a little translucent. Form a ball that is slightly smaller than a pea and pinch the top to give it a stalk.

Step 2: Using a pin, create lines to show the cloves inside the garlic.

Step 3: Carefully dust the tops with cream pastel, cut the top off the garlic stalk and dust with a little brown. Cut a tiny disc of the white clay mix and texture it with a cocktail stick, dust with some brown, then carefully press this on to the base of the garlic to form the root.

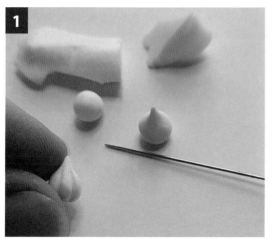

To begin forming the garlic, create a tiny drop shape.

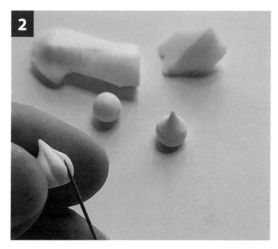

Using a pin, from tip to base press in lines to form the cloves of garlic.

Carefully pressing on the textured base of the garlic bulb to create the root, after forming and shading the tops. Garlic comes with a creamy coloured skin, but you can also blush the base with a little pink for some variety.

Tomato cane

Tomato canes can be quite tricky. It is important to add enough detail, while still keeping the cane simple enough that it looks good once it has been reduced in size.

You may want to use a real tomato to help with the choice of colours, but you will need a creamy white for the core, light yellow for the pips, a translucent and burgundy mix for the area around the pips, a light peachy pink for the shell and a red translucent mix for the skin. Try to keep the skin colour simple so that if you make whole tomatoes, it is easier to match the colour. Adding lots of translucent clay into each colour gives an overall juicy wet look to the finished cane.

Step 1: Start by making one half of the tomato. Form a semicircle in burgundy and cut slices into it for the lines that go out to the pips and holes to thread the pips into.

Step 2: Once you have put the pips through the holes and the white lines are in place, add a semicircle of white for the core.

Step 3: Hold the semicircular disc of clay between your finger and thumb, then press the edges while turning the disc to compress the tomato half evenly. By applying pressure, make the disc smaller

Starting by making one half of a tomato.

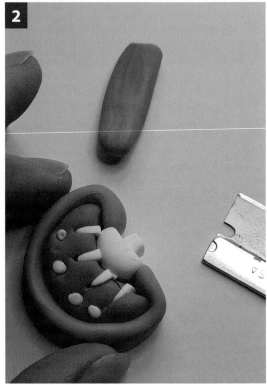

After positioning all the colours, you will have a half slice of tomato.

and thicker. Once it is half the size and twice as thick, cut it into two pieces. Add a little more of the flesh colour to fill any gaps and bind the two halves with a ribbon of skin colour around the outside

Step 4: Compress the tomato so that it gets smaller and fatter. Once it is long enough, you can begin to pull and draw out the cane and then roll it. You may need to cut the cane into a few workable lengths and keep pulling and rolling until it is nice and round and about the diameter of a pea for a regular tomato and smaller for a cherry tomato.

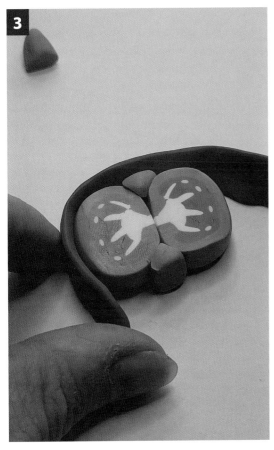

After putting the two halves of tomato together to make a round slice, add a thin layer of skin colour before pulling the cane fully.

After baking the pulled canes, the colours will become much more see-through as the translucent clay changes colour.

Black olive cane

To make black olive cane, simply roll a little black and translucent clay mix around a piece of unwrapped florists' wire and bake on the wire. After it is baked and cool, use pliers to remove the wire and cut the cane into little olive slices.

CREATING PIZZAS

Pizzas come in all kinds of shapes and sizes so choose whichever you prefer. Here I am using a base about the size of a 1/12 dinner plate for a medium pizza. To create a pizza base, you will need a pastry mix of white clay with the tiniest bit of yellow and caramel brown.

Step 1: Roll the clay into a ball, then flat with your finger. Use a round-ended modelling tool to push up a crust around the edge. Texture the crust using a toothbrush. Next, dry-brush browns to the crust, working from the bottom up as pizza browns from the bottom.

Step 2: Using some liquid polymer clay coloured with a few scrapings of reddish orange pastel, make a tomato sauce, then one coloured with creamy white pastel for the cheese. Spread and swirl a little of these over the base. It is a good idea to bake the pizza before adding the toppings, as the colour sometimes bleeds from the sauce into the toppings.

Step 3: Once baked and cool, add a little clear liquid polymer and whichever toppings you like before re-baking. The mushrooms and onions used in the pictures are also made using the caning method. After your pizzas have been baked, use lots of varnish to make them look really shiny and delicious.

Dry-brushing brown and golden shades of pastel on to the pastry-mix pizza bases gives them a baked look.

Using liquid clay to make tomato sauce and liquid cheese for the bases of the pizzas.

3

Lots of combinations of toppings and sizes for your pizzas, now all baked and varnished.

Pepperoni

Pepperoni and salami are fairly easy canes to begin with, although because of how they are made they are never the same twice. Have a look at a picture of the sausage you want to make, as the colours are a bit different for each type – pepperoni is more orange, while salami has more pink tones.

Step 1: Place together pieces of the appropriate colours for your sausage, for example various browns with orange, yellow and a touch of white or translucent. Basic meat colour is white and burgundy mixed with dark brown. Using your single-sided razor, cut all the colours together into even-sized pieces. Keep re-chopping until it is the texture you want.

Step 2: Press all the bits into a baton and roll and stretch to form the sausage cane. Bake the cane before slicing to keep the pieces round. Cut slices as required. You could add a very thin layer of white to create a skin for the sausage, texturing it with sandpaper.

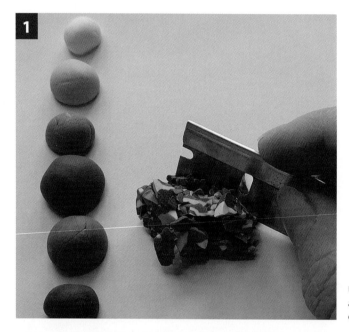

Using the chopping technique to cut and mix all the colours, creating a salami/pepperoni effect with the clay.

Cutting slices as required from your sausage baton.

Pepper Slices

Sliced peppers are a colourful addition to pizza, salad or even paella. It is quite simple to make a few different colours at once and have them ready to add to your projects.

Step 1: mix the colour of your choice with some translucent clay and press into a thin sheet. Do the same with some translucent clay with a little white mixed in. Press the sheets together.

Step 2: take three bamboo barbecue skewers and tape them together with sticky tape for form a triangle. Now wrap your slay sheets around the skewers, pushing it into the indentations to create a pepper shape. Bake them on the skewer and then slide them off ready for cutting.

Coloured and translucent clay wrapped around barbecue skewers to form a pepper shape.

Lots of different canes to make toppings for your pizza.

CHAPTER 5

Classic Roasts

· · · · · · · · · · · · ·

Making a large roast as a centrepiece for your table or kitchen creates the look of a celebration. Adding all the decorations and vegetables gives colour and impact. Cookbooks and supermarket magazines are a great source of ideas on how to style your roast dishes.

In this chapter, we are going to use some layering and cutting techniques to create meat dishes. Once you have made the basic meat pieces you can dress them with all kinds of vegetables, herbs and side dishes to create a real centrepiece. Use your miniature serving dish to help with scale, but leave room for the extras. All meats, whether raw or cooked, use a basic colour mix of burgundy, dark brown and caramel brown. For raw meats add translucent with a tiny bit of white, and for cooked use more white in the mix. Mixing these colours in different proportions creates different types of meat.

What would Sunday lunch be without a good old-fashioned roast?

ROAST TURKEY

Step 1: To make the meat for the turkey we use the meat mix (*see* above), but with very little of the coloured clays so as to leave it pale. The skin is a mix of translucent with a tiny bit of caramel brown. Wrap a thin layer of skin around the meat and form a roll. Stretch the roll so that it is fat at one end and thinner at the other.

Step 2: Using a serving dish as a guide, create a heart-shaped body then drumsticks and long, thin wings with the roll of clay, pulling out to the thickness you need.

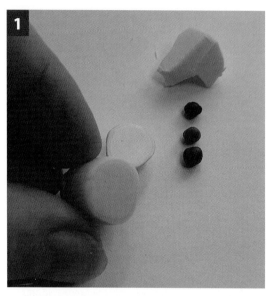

The colours of clay used to make the meat and skin of the turkey, which starts as a simple cane.

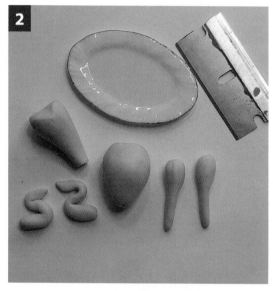

Dividing up the baton of clay into the pieces that will form the turkey.

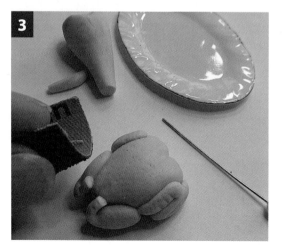

Texturing the skin of the assembled turkey by pressing with sandpaper to create dimples in the skin.

Dry-brushing on shades of brown and golden yellow give the turkey a roasted look.

Step 3: Assemble the turkey, legs at the thin end of the body and wings at the top bent into as 'S' shape. Once you are happy with the shape of the bird, press an indentation from the head end down the spine to create the breasts. Texture the bird using sandpaper or a toothbrush, pressing lines around the ankles and on the wings.

Step 4: Use the regular baking colours of brown and golden yellow to add roast colour, concentrating on working up the sides and on the top.

Step 5: Add varnish to the baked turkey to give a shiny, juicy look.

Adding varnish to the skin after the piece is baked gives it a shiny, juicy look.

Different birds

By using a darker meat mix and changing the shape of the bird, you can make ducks, geese or whatever you wish. To texture a goose, I use a piece of fine net, the same as used to texture fish later on. If you wish to create a carved turkey, this is best done after the turkey has been baked but is still warm so as to achieve a more natural look. Carving tiny strips gives a good, slightly ragged effect.

You can choose to carve the turkey after it has been baked while it is still warm and soft, as this gives a more natural shredded appearance to the meat inside. If you don't like turkey, you could make goose or duck instead.

ROAST LAMB

To create a leg of lamb, use the basic meat mix (*see above*), but with a little more colour. This may take a few attempts to get right – looking at a reference photo is a good idea.

Step 1: Create a roll using a meat mix and the same skin mix as for the turkey, then form it into a rough leg shape. Make a little roll of cream-coloured clay, slice off a circle and use it to make a bone at both ends of the leg. Use a rounded tool to make an indentation in the end of the bone.

Step 2: Use your razor blade to slice off some thin sheets of skin to create the effect that the meat has been trimmed.

Step 3: On the cut end of the leg use a toothpick to scratch the texture of cut meat; any slices of meat can be textured in this way, with scratches scraped diagonally across the meat's surface.

Step 4: Dry-brush a little red to the centre of the cut area and some browns to the outside of the meat, for a roasted colour.

Step 5: After baking the piece, varnish it and whilst the varnish is wet, you can add some garnish, herbs, peppers, or whatever you choose. I have used some dark brown and green scenic scatter and a few little green strips of clay as herbs.

Using a basic meat mix to create the base colour for your roast lamb: clays in white, dark brown, burgundy and caramel brown.

Using a small brush to dry-brush a little red into the centre of the assembled leg of lamb gives it a natural rare look, but add it just a little at a time.

After baking and varnishing, add a little scenic scatter or coloured pencil shavings to give the appearance of a herby crust to the roast.

BEEF WELLINGTON

Step 1: To make the beef, mix a similar shade of meat mix to the lamb, then form it into a roll.

Step 2: Make the paté layer by chopping together some cream, black, green and brown shades of clay and wrapping them around the beef roll.

Step 3: Add a thin layer of pastry mix to make the final piece neat. Standard pastry mix is white with a tiny bit of yellow and caramel (*see* Chapter 2). Roll the baton of clay until it reaches the desired thickness, using your miniature dinner plate as a guide.

Step 4: To make the lattice pastry, use the corner of your razor blade to cut tiny, even lines in thinly rolled pastry mix, then cut a second line below in the alternate spaces between the cuts above. Keep doing this to cover the pastry,

then carefully stretch it to open the gaps. Choose a good section of this and press it on to your Wellington.

Step 5: Tidy the end by slicing it off, then texture the meat and rough up the paté with a cocktail stick. Drawing the stick across the meat in rough stripes makes a good meat texture. Dry-brush a little red to the centre of the meat and baked colour to the pastry, starting from the base and brushing across the lattice to highlight the edges and give a golden-brown baked appearance.

Step 6: Once baked, varnish the surface to give it a lovely sheen. Garnish with vegetables of your choice. This project also looks great with salmon instead of the beef.

Using the meat mix, the chopped mushroom layer and the pastry to build the layers of the Beef Wellington.

Using a medium soft brush to add a baked colour to highlight the lattice and some red to give the centre of the meat a rare look.

6

The finished Beef Wellington looks great served on an oval plate or wooden board and after baking the lattice looks lovely when varnished and shiny.

CHAPTER 6

Butcher's Window

. . . .

This section reminds me of the tiny butcher's shop in the town where I live. It has a traditional window hanging with chickens, rabbits and legs of lamb and the curious lawn of plastic grass with pork chops lying around in rows on it.

In this section we are going to make some raw meat items, then use them in different ways in a range of grocery ideas. These pieces are great to display on wooden or marble slabs and with knives and cleavers. It is possible to make meat hooks using wire and a nice bit of blood by either colouring some varnish or texture gel with pastels. For this project we will be using the meat mix from Chapter 2, but with transparent clay with just a tiny bit of white as the base.

RAW CHICKEN

To make a chicken use the same technique as with the turkey (*see* Chapter 5), but making the bird a bit smaller and skinnier; use a miniature baking dish or chopping board to help with the scale.

Step 1: Using a photo as a guide, mix together the burgundy, brown, caramel and a tiny amount of white clays with translucent to make the flesh colour. Remember that translucent clay looks more opaque before it is baked, so your mix may appear a bit pinker than it will end up.

Step 2: A 2:1 mix of translucent and white clay makes a good skin layer. Roll the skin flat and wrap it around the flesh colour to create a baton.

Step 3: Form pieces of the baton into the heart shape of the body of the chicken and then two drumsticks and two long thin wings with pointed ends formed into an 'S' shape.

Step 4: Press the legs and wings of the bird in place and add a dent to show the spine. Texture the bird with sandpaper, using a toothpick in hard to reach areas.

Step 5: From this bird, you can choose to leave it whole or cut it into sections as you might do for cooking or packaging. You can see from the picture that after baking the pieces, the flesh colour shows through more to give a jelly-like appearance.

Using a raw meat mix with more translucent than white in the mix for the flesh, and a skin mix of translucent, white and a touch of caramel.

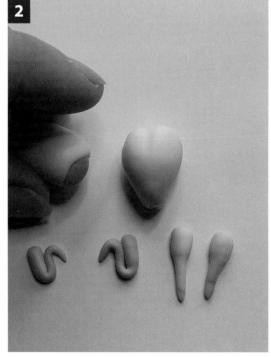

From the baton of clay, forming the shapes that will create whole chickens and chicken pieces.

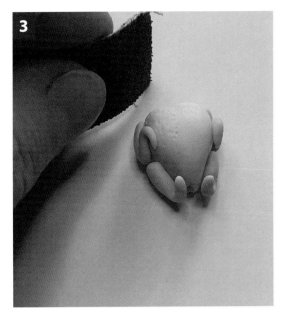

Using sandpaper to tap on the dimpled texture of the raw chicken skin.

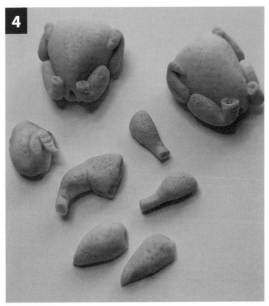

The unbaked pieces and whole chickens.

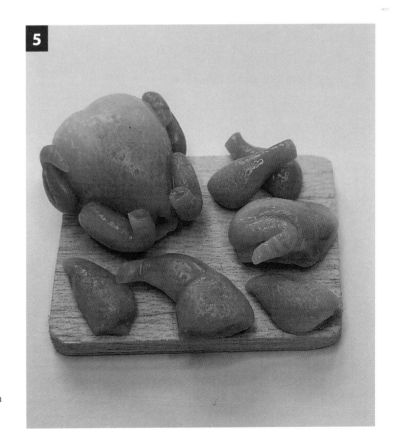

Once baked and varnished, the skin becomes more see-through and the flesh colour inside begins to show through. Dabbing off the varnish with a tissue allows the texture to be seen again whilst keeping it shiny.

RACK OF LAMB

Step 1: For the rack of lamb, first make a cane using the meat mix from the chicken project above, but coloured a little darker. Follow the same recipe for the skin mix. Use a thin sheet of the skin mix to create a seam of fat in the meat by cutting the meat mix in half and sandwiching the fat piece in between.

Step 2: Pull and lengthen the cane whilst pressing it into a teardrop shape.

Step 3: To create bones sticking up, cut out little sections of the cane with the razor blade, using a toothpick to help. If you are just making chops, you don't need to do this.

Step 4: To give the meat a trimmed appearance, use the razor blade to skim off pieces of the skin so that the meat colour shows through. Texture the meat using a cocktail stick, creating a scratched effect.

Step 5: From the original cane, you can make whole racks of lamb or lamb chops, or both. If you need a bit of blood on your chops, mix a little pastel colour into some liquid clay, or apply this later to the finished piece with coloured varnish.

Creating fat lines in the meat gives a more natural appearance.

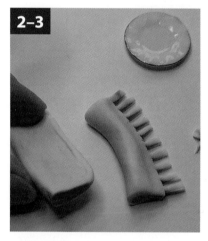

Pulling the cane and creating the shape of the rack of lamb before cutting in the bone shapes.

Using a single-sided razor to slice off patches of the fat layer gives a realistic texture to the meat.

From the cane you can make either whole racks of lamb or lamb chops, or a mixture of both.

BACON

Bacon is a really fun cane to make and if you store it unbaked in a plastic bag it can be used for lots of projects, such as breakfasts, burgers and pigs in blankets. In this section I have made streaky and back bacon.

Step 1: Make up a few different colours of raw meat mix and to each add a little more white because bacon looks a bit more cooked than other raw meats. Make up the same 2:1 skin mix as for raw chicken.

Step 2: Press out the pieces of meat mix and layer them with skin mix to create a block of layers.

Step 3: Wrap one or both sides with skin mix.

Step 4: Squash and pull the cane to make it long and flat. A miniature plate will help you to work out how long the bacon pieces should be.

Step 5: When you decide to use the bacon, cut thin slices and use a round-ended tool to make the slices crinkly and to define the layers.

Using different shades of meat mix for the bacon, somewhere between raw and cooked in colour.

Creating the stripes and patches in the bacon by layering colours with fat in between.

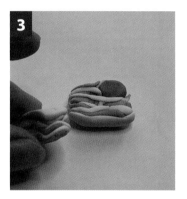

Back bacon has larger patches of colour than streaky bacon, but both canes are a flat, rectangular shape.

Slicing bacon canes is great fun – never expect two of them to be the same.

Using a round-ended tool to texture the slices of bacon and make the edges a bit frilly before baking.

Using the bacon slices as part of a British classic breakfast.

Making kebabs

By using leftover pieces from your meat project and some hoop-ended jewellery findings or wire, it is easy to make kebabs for the barbecue. Layer the meat slices with some vegetables from other projects. Little round tomatoes add a pop of colour.

Using jewellery findings to create kebabs from leftover pieces of clay.

CHAPTER 7

Medieval Feasts

· · · · · · · · · · · · · · · · ·

n this section we will be using a few differ-ent techniques to make some extravagant dishes fit for a royal feast. Looking at some of the pictures of food from this time it's all about showing off and creating huge displays of food, such as whole roasted boar and peacocks decorated with fruits, vegetables and feathers.

Choosing a specific period means that it is a good idea to research what foods existed at the time and what would be historically accurate. In these projects I have avoided foods that were not around in medieval Europe, such as potatoes, orange carrots and tomatoes, and used things like turnips, plums and apples.

Sweets in all sorts of shapes used to make moulds for pies and puddings with silicone moulding medium.

◀ A pig's head ready for a medieval feast.

RAISED PIE

For this pie you can use a mould or model by hand. I have used moulds made from little sweets, although small lids would also work.

Step 1: Using a cooked meat mix in a few shades, plus some translucent with a little white for the fat, chop the pieces together to make the pie filling.

Step 2: With a pastry mix of white with a little yellow and caramel wrap the meat filling to make a cane.

Step 3: Close over the top of the cane and slice off a piece to push into the mould. Chill in the fridge to make the pie easier to remove.

Step 4: Carefully remove the pie from the mould and add some trim, plaits and leaves for decoration, plus a steam hole in the top.

Step 5: Dry-brush on some baked colour, starting at the base and brushing across the decoration to highlight it.

Step 6: After baking the pie, it can be cut to show the filling. Model-makers' foam can be coloured to look like herbs on the serving board.

A simple pie mix is made using the chopping method to combine the colours of clay.

Making a cane by wrapping a pastry mix around the meat filling, then closing over the top of the cane and slicing off a piece to push into the mould.

Decorating the pie with crimps, plaits and leaves made from the pastry mix and pushing holes in the top for the steam to escape. Golden brown colours add a baked look to the pie and make the decoration stand out.

The finished, baked pie is presented on a serving dish, varnished and served with plums, which are not varnished so that they have a dewy bloom on the skin.

ROAST PIG'S HEAD

This project is a bit of a test of your modelling skills. It is a good idea to have a reference photo of a pig's head – a bit gory but that's medieval cooking for you. Also use your serving dish to help with scale.

Step 1: The mix for the pig's head is a skin mix of translucent, a little white and caramel; all of the other colour is painted on later. Form this mix into a drop shape with a long nose and fat neck underneath.

Step 2: Following a reference photo create semicircles for the ears, folding them over slightly.

Press on the snout, eyes and wrinkles with a small ball tool. This may take a while until you are happy with the positioning, but because you have only used one colour you can reshape as much as you need. It is tempting to model the pig as we assume they look, that is, a round head with a button for a nose, but the shape of a pig's head is more like that of a dog and this is where the reference photo really helps.

Step 3: Using red, brown and dark brown, start gently layering on the colour. This will really bring the little pig to life.

Using the pale raw skin mix create a drop shape that fits nicely on to your serving dish for the head of the pig.

Pressing on semicircular shapes to create ears for the pig.

Colouring the folds and wrinkles in the skin and adding a blush of pink colour around the nose, eyes and ears brings the piece to life.

The final head baked and presented on an elaborate dish with vegetables that would have been available in the medieval period, such as apples, onions and turnips.

Suckling pig

The head of the suckling pig on a spit is made a bit smaller and has a body added. Making this on the piece of wire helps you to avoid squashing the pig while you are modelling it. Form the body of the pig by threading on a baton of clay and adding arms and legs. Again, work from a reference photo to see how the legs bend and finish them with slits in the feet for trotters. Create the shapes of hips and shoulders using the round-ended tool and don't forget the curly tail. Colouring this with a bit more of the brown shades around the feet and belly, then adding lots of varnish after it has been baked makes the pig appear roasted. This would look great over a large open fire.

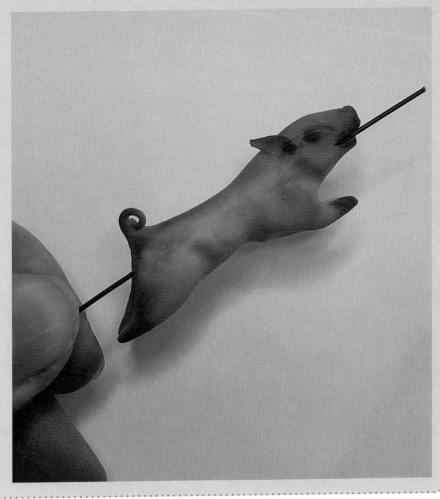

Having the suckling pig on a stick from the start helps you to work on it from all angles and will be needed later to display it roasting over the fire or bonfire.

PEACOCK FEATHERS

These make a great decoration for a banqueting table and they are quite easy to make using white feathers and permanent markers. Use a reference photo to help with the colours.

Step 1: Make sure to use the front of the feather as the back doesn't take colour as well. Start from the centre with the eye of the feather and be gentle because the ink spreads. Work outwards using stripes of colour in the direction the feather naturally goes.

Step 2: Using some fine nail scissors, trim the feather to create the right shape and snip into the lower parts of the feather to make it a bit ragged.

I have put my feathers with a roast peacock, which is actually a repurposed Christmas goose made in the same way as the roast turkey in the 'Classic Roasts' chapter. The feathers also would be good just as a display in a vase in a Victorian-style house, or you could try a taxidermy peacock if you are feeling adventurous.

Adding coloured pen to the feathers very gently as it has a habit of spreading. The colour goes on best on the front of the feather.

Using nail scissors to cut a smaller feather out of the larger one.

A roast peacock, displayed on a grand serving dish.

CHAPTER 8

Retro Party Food

. . . .

This chapter reminds me of birthday and drinks parties in the 1970s when the more colourful the food was, the better, and everyone was beginning to recreate a bit of glamour at home. We are going to create some colourful and fun party treats from that era.

We are going to use resin or a similar product to create the jelly. I have used powder from the coloured chalk pastels to dye the resin, which works really well as long as you give it a good long stir to melt all the little bits of coloured powder. Resin in a mould gives a good result with nice crisp edges. Jelly moulds can be bought quite easily, or you can make a mould either by hand from a mounded clay shape or from something like a button or a lid.

The other new medium being used in this project is artists' acrylic texture gel. This is usually used in acrylic painting to create a thicker paint or textured surface. It is best to get the translucent type so that you can use it for different-coloured projects. It sets solid in 24 hours and makes great cream, icing or custard on things that can't be baked, like resin or things you have previously baked. You can buy it from artists' supply shops or online.

The prawn cocktail is a retro party classic, served in a martini glass.

PRAWN COCKTAIL

A sophisticated 1980s starter originally, piled high and served in a Martini glass.

Step 1: Mix different shades as shown to make a blended colour for the lettuce and a striped block for the prawns. For both, use translucent with a touch of white to start, then for the green add a little more to each piece to build up the colour gently, while for the pink the colour is added in larger amounts so that the stripes are obvious.

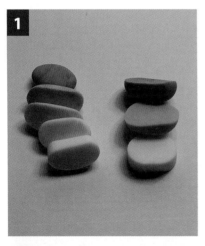

Using different shades of colour to create either graduated or striped colours for the lettuce and prawns.

Using soft clay to create a mould of the inside of a delicate Martini glass.

Step 2: Because I have chosen to use delicate Martini glasses for my prawn cocktail and would rather not risk baking them to fire the clay, I have made a mould to work in instead. If you are using plastic glasses this will also be necessary. Take the shape of the glass with a piece of soft clay, then bake it to create a mould to use for the final pieces.

Step 3: Layer the colours and pull them out into lettuce and prawn canes, which can then be cut into thin slices. Use a ball-ended tool to texture the lettuce leaves.

Step 4: Make the prawns by slicing tiny striped sticks of the pink mix, rolling them a little and curling to make a prawn shape.

Step 5: Line the mould with some slices of tomato (*see* Chapter 4), then build up a base of lettuce leaves. A little blob of liquid clay in the centre will hold it all together as you work.

Step 6: The Marie Rose sauce is made by mixing liquid clay with the pastel colours shown. You will need to add white to the mix as the clay will become more translucent as it bakes. Apply the sauce with a cocktail stick and build up a good mix of sauce and prawns in the mould to make it look really appetising.

Using a ball-ended tool to build up the salad in the mould out of thin strips of lettuce, tomato and prawns before baking.

6

Mixing the Marie Rose sauce using liquid clay and pastel colour.

Fixing the prawn cocktail

To stick the prawn cocktail into its glass, use a dot of clear glue. Alternatively, use a small piece of sticky tack if you might want to remove the cocktail later and make a Martini instead. I would not advise using superglue because it leaves a cloudy film over the glass when it dries. While this can be wiped off, in this case it will not be reachable inside the glass.

A wedge of lemon finishes off the prawn cocktail nicely.

SWISS ROLL AND BATTENBERG CAKE

Two fabulous old-fashioned cakes that can be used for lots of projects. the Battenburg cake was invented in Europe in the nineteenth century to celebrate a royal wedding and is really pretty with its pink and yellow sponge.

Both of these projects are made using the caning technique, and for real retro school-dinner nostalgia the Swiss roll can easily be made into an Arctic roll, or for Christmas a chocolate yule log. Both cakes can also be rolled and stretched to make much smaller scale pieces; in the picture they are displayed on a 1/12 and 1/24 size plate. Slightly bigger and they could be individual cakes for a lunch box or cake stand.

Swiss roll

Step 1: Make up some light pastry mix with white, yellow and caramel and some jam using translucent and red.

Step 2: Press both mixes out flat, with the cake colour thicker than the jam, then roll them to create the swirl. As this is a cane, you can roll it to any width you need; about the width of a pencil for 1/12, smaller for mini-rolls, and roughly the width of a barbecue skewer for 1/24.

Step 3: Using sandpaper or a toothbrush, texture the top and ends of the roll.

Step 4: Dry-brush some baked colour on to the roll. Cut to length and slice as needed. Texture your cut ends and bake in the oven. Once cooked, dab on some white acrylic paint for the icing sugar.

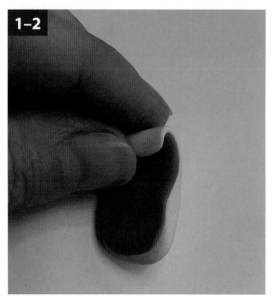

A thick layer of pastry-mix-coloured clay with a thin layer of red are rolled up together to make a jam Swiss roll with a swirl in the centre.

Dabbing the surface with sandpaper to add the spongy texture.

Battenberg cake

Battenberg is a lovely cake to make and not as hard as it looks.

Step 1: Mix some lovely pastel colours for the cake, white for the icing and translucent yellow with a little white and caramel for the marzipan.

Step 2: Make the pink and yellow cake pieces into four batons, then wrap each in a very thin sheet of white.

Step 3: Wrap all four batons in a sheet of the marzipan colour and roll it a little to stick everything together. Press each side of the wrapped baton on the work surface to make it square, ensuring that the cake pieces are in the right place.

Step 4: Stretch your square baton into a long cane by carefully pulling it and running it through your fingers to keep its square shape.

Step 5: Only the ends of this cake and any slices will need texturing with a toothpick.

The pale-coloured sponge sections ready to create the Battenberg cake.

The four batons of clay placed carefully together and surrounded by a layer of marzipan, ready to pull into a square cane.

The finished cane can be cut into slices and textured.

Cakes for all kinds of teatime projects as well as cake shops, cafés and to use in trifle.

SHERRY TRIFLE

When I was little, no celebration at my grandmother's house was ever without a sherry-filled trifle, sometimes with strawberries or mandarins inside and always with sprinkles, cherries and silver balls on top.

Step 1: Mix the resin, colouring it with pastel powder. Pour into your chosen bowls, leaving room for the custard, and push in the Swiss roll slices, or fruit if you prefer.

Placing baked slices of Swiss roll into a coloured resin jelly base while still wet.

Layering a custard-coloured topping of texture gel and acrylic paint on the set resin jelly.

Using a tiny star-shaped piping nozzle, pipe white texture gel straight on to baking paper.

Topping with a layer of white texture gel before adding the piped cream stars.

Step 2: Once the resin has set, mix some texture gel with a little white acrylic paint and colour with pastel powder to make it yellow. Layer this on top of the jelly.

Step 3 To make the cream swirls, create a mix of half and half texture gel and acrylic paint. You need a tiny star piping nozzle and a small plastic bag. Cut the corner off the bag, push the nozzle through and fill the bag with the gel mix. Pipe the stars on to baking paper so that they peel off easily when dry. If any of your stars are particularly good, you could make a mould so that you can make cream swirls more easily in future. If you are feeling brave,

you could pipe straight on to your cream layer, but piping on to a wet gel layer is tricky, and this way you can choose only the best ones for your trifles.

Step 4: Put a layer of cream on top of the custard layer. You can save the cream used for piping by sealing up the bag so that it won't dry. Add the cream swirls and push them into the cream layer a little so that they stick.

Step 5: You can decorate the trifles as I have done, with sprinkles made from hair-thin pieces of clay baked and cut into little bits, but cherries (*see* Chapter 13) or almonds (*see* Chapter 12) would be good too.

5

Finishing off with sprinkles made from tiny threads of baked clay and a layer of varnish once everything has set.

GREEN JELLO SALAD

This extraordinary 1950s American classic consists of bright green Jello filled with all kinds of unlikely salad ingredients. The Jello salad is created using resin, rather than clay. I used a regular dolls' house jelly mould to make an unbaked clay jelly, then pushed it in the middle to make it bundt-shaped. I then baked the new shape and took a mould from it when it had cooled.

Step 1: Mix the resin according to the instructions on your brand and colour it with green pastel powder. Pour the resin into the mould and add your chosen ingredients, pushing them down with a cocktail stick.

Step 2: After the resin has been setting for a while and is getting thick, adjust the placement of the prawns and olives, etc, if they have moved.

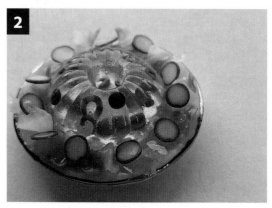

The set Jello salad is varnished to make it extra see-through and sits on a bed of lettuce.

Resin coloured with green pastel in a jelly or bundt cake mould creates the Jello base for the salad.

Jello salad ingredients

The prawns and lettuce in this Jello salad are from the prawn cocktail project above. The stuffed olives are made by wrapping some olive-green clay around a baton of red clay rolled to about the width of a barbecue skewer, then baked and sliced. You could, of course, add whatever ingredients you like to your Jello salad, such as tomatoes, peppers and pineapple – it seems that anything goes in this amazing dish.

Using leftovers

When working with resin there always seem to be leftovers, so use any jelly, cake or pie moulds you have to make jellies. Adding some leftover fruit slices to the jellies looks effective. Once you have a few, you can pile them to make grand Victorian-style jellies and puddings.

Leftover resin can be popped into moulds to make all kinds of simple jellies and desserts.

CHAPTER 9

Fruit Bowl

· · · · · · · ·

The first dolls' house object I owned was a bowl of fruit. It was in a tiny willow-patterned bowl and was made from a block of plaster with the fruit carved out and coloured. Making a fruit bowl is an excellent project as it gives you the opportunity to try lots of different techniques and create something that looks great in your dolls' house, or makes a lovely present for a dolls' house fan. Making a few of each type of fruit means you can use them for other projects, like a crate of bananas or a bucket of apples. They can also be added to pies and tarts in the kitchen. The types of fruit you choose are entirely up to you, but make sure they fit with the era and style of your house. If you choose to create a shop or market stall, however, all types of fruit are on offer.

Lots of tiny fruit looks great in the dolls' house kitchen, dining room or even on a little market stall.

APPLES

Apples are such a varied fruit that you can experiment with different sizes, shapes and colours. We will be using both dry-brushing and wet-brushing in this project. Choose the right style for your house – for example, if it is a country cottage you will want small greenish apples and large cooking varieties for pies. If your house is a grand mansion, you will need shiny red apples.

Step 1: The basic cane for all apples and pears is the same and by adding a skin you will be able to cut or peel the finished fruit. For the flesh, you will need translucent clay with a tiny amount of white, yellow and green. For the skin, a half-and-half mix of translucent and white, again with yellow and green added. Form the flesh colour into a baton shape and wrap a very thin layer of the skin colour around it. Roll this into a long cane.

Step 2: Cut pea-sized pieces from the cane and fold in the ends to form a ball covered with the skin colour.

Step 3: The base of each apple must pinched into a point as apples are fattest at the top and taper in at the base. For pears, roll the pieces in your fingers to form a drop shape. For a cooking apple, a simple ball shape is fine. Using a cocktail stick, a fine ball-ended tool or both, create star-shaped dents in the top of the apples for the stalks. When baking, stand apples pointed end down on the baking tile and pears pointed end up.

Step 4: Using some images of apples to help, start to colour the apples. First, with a medium-sized

Forming the apple shape using a cane by closing each end to create a ball completely wrapped in skin colour.

Apples come in different shapes and sizes and by creating a drop shape, they become pears.

Adding blushes of colour to different areas on the apples and blushes of brown and green on the pears.

Fine-detailing the apples and pears and creating a darker area inside the star-shaped indentations for the stalks.

soft brush add blushes of green from the bottom up, then blushes of red on the fattest part of the apple. Using a smaller soft brush add some blushes of brown in the stalk hole and for the pears on the sides of the fruit.

Step 5: Using a fine-pointed wet brush, paint on some fine red lines over the red-blushed areas. With the same brush and some wet brown pastel, accentuate the star shape with a few lines and add some spots on the pears.

Stalks

Before storing or baking apples and pears, I make stalks using tiny pieces of brown button thread attached with liquid clay. These will be fine during the baking process. Clay can also be used for stalks, but they can be a bit brittle after baking because they are so thin.

Each apple is different and that's fine. Adding stalks made from button thread and the odd leaf makes them even more real.

ORANGES

Oranges are a fairly easy fruit to start with, but do need a few little tricks to make them look realistic.

Step 1: Make a mix using translucent clay to give a juicy look, with some white, orange and yellow added. The mix will be a little lighter than your finished orange.

Step 2: Roll balls of clay about the size of a pea on a piece of sandpaper to give a dimpled texture.

Step 3: Using a cocktail stick, push a tiny star-shaped dent into the end of each orange and push in a tiny circle of leaf-green clay to form a calyx.

Step 4: Using a medium-sized soft brush, add a blush of orange-red to the sides of each orange. You can either bake the oranges separately or ready arranged in a fruit bowl, stuck into place with some liquid clay.

Using sandpaper to texture and shape your oranges.

Creating a star-shaped indentation in the end of each orange and adding a tiny circle of clay for a calyx.

PEACHES

Peaches are a really pretty fruit to make and whilst you may varnish the other fruits you have made once they are finished, whole peaches are best kept matt for a soft, velvety look.

Step 1: The mix is simply translucent clay, with a little white and golden yellow; no skin is needed for these. Roll pea-sized pieces into balls, then pinch a tiny point at one end and create a dent at the other end with a cocktail stick and a dent forming a line down one side of the peach to about half way down.

Step 2: This next part really makes the peach look real. If the place where you are working is quite warm, it may help to put your peaches in the fridge for a while to firm up. Start with an all-over blush of golden yellow using a medium-sized soft brush, then add some blushes of red on the fattest parts of the fruit and finally smaller blushes of purple in the centre of the red blushes where the fruit is really ripe.

Step 3: If you would like to cut a few of your peaches and add stones, this is the moment. Texture the place where the stone will go and give it a little blush of purple with a small brush. A tiny piece of brown clay makes the stone to place in one half. Because of all the translucent clay in the peach mix, the inside looks really juicy, with a bit of colour, a stone and a final coat of varnish after it's baked.

Creating the look of skin with blushes of yellow, red and purple pastel.

Adding a stone to half of a cut peach.

BANANAS

Step 1: To start making a bunch of bananas you will need a mix of white and yellow with a small amount of translucent clay to make the mix flexible but still opaque. Use a dinner plate to help with sizing the bananas. Once you have made some baton shapes, pinch the end to a point and press the sides of the banana on the work surface to make the baton more square. Roll the top of each banana between your fingers to form a stalk.

Step 2: For a single banana, just cut the top of the stalk and bend the banana a little, but for a bunch arrange the bananas together. I have used five bananas as they fit nicely together. Roll all the stalks together between your finger and thumb to form one stalk and cut this off close to the fruit.

Step 3: To colour the banana, we will use both wet- and dry-brushing techniques. Again, it is a good idea to look at a real banana before adding lines and spots. Using a medium-sized soft brush, add a blush of green to both ends of the banana. Then with a smaller brush, add a blush of brown before using the fine wet brush to add some dark brown colour to the stalk and a few lines and spots down the sides at the places where the skin would open when peeled. Some of these can be faded and done with dry pastel powder and some made stronger; you can use a marker pen also for these. Bunches of bananas also look great in crates lined with blue or purple tissue.

Giving the banana its signature shape – flattening the sides slightly creates a more square shape.

Bringing the bananas to life with fine detailing.

STRAWBERRY CANES

This is extremely useful cane to have to hand. It can be used in so many projects, such as cakes, pies, summer puddings, preserves and drinks. I always bake lots of short canes when I make this one, so that I can keep the shape of the strawberry the same all the way through. It is, however, a fairly complicated design, so never turns out quite the same twice.

Step 1: Several colours and shades of clay will be needed: a light green; a red with a little white and translucent for the core of the strawberry; white with a little cream and translucent for flexibility; a strong red with translucent for the skin; two more balls of the same red, but with increasing amounts of white added to make them a pinker tone.

Step 2: Create a heart shape for the core of the strawberry and add a triangle of the cream colour to the top of the heart. Surround it with a strip of cream colour. Add the green to the top and then layers of the red, starting with the palest – don't add the darkest skin colour yet.

Step 3: Cut through the sides of the strawberry to insert pieces of the cream colour, creating rays coming out from the core of the strawberry.

Step 4: Once these are all in, wrap the final skin colour around the whole strawberry.

Step 5: Now that we have the large cane, we have to stretch it to make it smaller, while maintaining the pattern inside. Using the finger and thumb of both hands, slowly turn the cane while pressing it inwards. The cane will start to get more compact

All the colours to create a strawberry cane, with lots of translucent clay mixed in to make the strawberry slices look juicy.

Assembling the colours in layers to form a heart shape at the centre of the strawberry slice.

and longer. As it gets longer, pull and stroke the cane downwards.

Step 6: Once the cane is reasonably long, cut it into more manageable lengths and keep pulling.

Once the canes are the desired size, pinch them to form the triangle shape of the strawberry slice and check that everything is where it should be inside the cane. These canes store well after baking.

Using pressure on all sides of the completed large cane to begin to shrink and elongate it, while keeping the centre pattern in place.

Finished canes cut to a manageable length and squeezed to create a heart shape can be baked for cutting later.

Using the baked strawberry canes for all kinds of baking and decorating projects.

FIG CANES

The fig cane is a nice, unusual cane and can be used in sweet and savoury projects – for example, it looks great on a cheese board.

Step 1: The clays you will need are: a mix of translucent and dark red for the empty core of the fig; translucent, red, dark red and a little white for the main flesh colour; a cream colour for the next layer and the pips; and translucent, purple, dark red and black for the skin colour, but mixed less well so as to make it a bit marbled.

Step 2: Making the large fig shape starts with a rough star in the centre consisting of the dark red and translucent mix. Using half of the cream colour and the flesh colour create a baton with a white core and red around the edge. Roll this baton until it is quite long, then cut it into pieces, fitting them around the star. These are the pips of the fig. Surround this with the rest of the cream clay.

Step 3: With finger and thumbs of both hands begin to compress and pull the cane. Once it is half the size and reasonably long, wrap a very thin layer of the black skin around the baton and continue to pull it into a long cane. Once the cane is the required size, cut it into manageable lengths and form a point along the top of each cane for the stalk. Fig canes are best stored unbaked and wrapped in plastic as they look best with a bit of texturing.

All the colours needed to make the seeds at the centre of the fig and its lovely dark skin.

Fitting together all the little canes to make the seed texture inside the fig, the white layer and the dark purply skin.

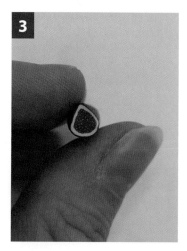
Pinching the top of the fig cane to create the pointed top where the stalk is.

Half figs

If you would like to make some half figs rather than just slices, cut some fat slices from your cane and pinch one side of them closed in the same way as with the apples. Form a point on the top of the fig and cut it freshly at the open end to show the inside of the whole fig. After baking, I varnish the inside but not the outside of the fig. The exterior of the fig is a lovely streaky pattern and a few more delicate lines can be added after you have formed the rounded half fig.

Half figs look great served on a cheese board or as a dessert.

CHAPTER 10

Preserves

· · · · · · ·

This section is all about preserves, jams and jellies – beautiful little things in jars that look wonderful on the shelves of your dolls' house kitchen or shop. I am using lots of things that we have made already, resin for the liquid and various glass jars. Using resin in jars can sometimes cause them to break, so have a few spares to hand. I have also used a new product here for the blackberry jam and mustard seeds. Accent beads, or 'bead caviar', are used for nail art as well as craft and can be ordered online. They come in all sorts of colours and can be used for lots of miniature projects, such as silver balls for cake decoration, black for currants, clear for bubbles; the list goes on.

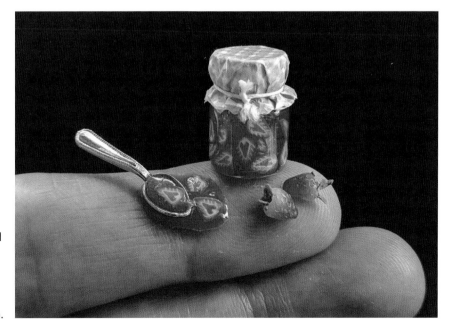

Bright and colourful jars of jam and pickles look like little gems on the shelves of your dolls' house kitchen.

ORANGE SLICES FOR MARMALADE

To make orange slices we are going to create a cane. This cane is a really useful one that can be used for all sorts of projects and once mastered can also be used to make lemons, limes, grapefruit and blood oranges.

Step 1: The colour mixes for the clay in this project start with a translucent clay cut into two larger pieces and one smaller. To the two larger pieces add some golden yellow clay and to one of them also some orange. To the smaller piece add the same, but then also some red. The quickest way to do this is to colour the whole batch yellow, break it in half and add the orange, then break that and add the red. You will also need a quantity of white mixed with a tiny piece of translucent to make it

Graduated shades of orange mixed with translucent clay give the cane a natural juicy look.

Creating a bull's-eye effect using layers of the different orange shades.

Cutting the disc into equal segments to create individual orange pieces.

Creating the lines of pith between each segment and the white spot in the centre of the orange slice.

Starting to compress the circle to make a cane.

Halfway through the process of pulling the cane the ends don't look great, but this is normal and the inside when cut should look like a perfect orange slice.

flexible and a strong orange colour for the skin. I have made the skin darker than when we made whole oranges because you only see a very small bit of it when the cane is sliced.

Step 2: Create a bull's eye shape with your colours. Don't worry too much about blending them, because as they are translucent-based they will blend themselves quite well when baked. Once the cane has been shrunk, there will be a subtle fading of colours.

Step 3: With your single-sided razor, slice the bull's eye into even segments.

Step 4: Take half of the white and press it into a long ribbon about as wide as the segments are thick. Cut the ribbon into pieces and fit them between each segment to create the lines of pith and the white spot in the centre of the orange slice. Press the whole thing together to make it one circle again.

Step 5: Wrap the circles in a thick layer of white and a thin layer of the orange skin colour. Start to pull the cane, by putting the circle between your finger and thumb and rotating it while pressing inwards. It should start to get smaller and longer, while maintaining the pattern of the segments inside.

Step 6: When the cane is about twice as thick as you want it, you can start to pull it by running your fingers along the length of the cane while still pulling gently. The ends at this point may not look promising, but inside the cane should be intact.

Step 7: Cut the cane into more manageable lengths as you go. When it is the size you want, slightly smaller than a pencil width for 1/12 scale, roll the canes on a piece of sandpaper to texture them.

In this project, I have chosen to bake some of the canes for slicing later, while keeping others unbaked in a plastic bag so that I can texture the inside of them later if I want. A cane like this is easily left larger for bigger-scale projects, or rolled smaller for 1/24 projects. The smaller size also makes good sweets.

Once the canes are at the right width they can be cut to usable lengths and the rough ends removed.

By changing the colours of clay and the width of the canes, you can make all kinds of different citrus fruit canes to use in various projects.

JELLY, JAM AND MARMALADE

Filling a jar

In this project, we will be using a two-part resin mixed as per the instructions on the packet.

Step 1: Once you have mixed the resin, transfer it to fill the jars to about two-thirds full, leaving room for the fruit. Scrape a little pastel colour into the jar and mix really well with a cocktail stick. Only add a little colour, as the fruit will also lend colour to the jam.

Step 2: Once you have decided on the flavour of your jams, add the pre-baked fruit, such as lemons, cherries, rhubarb or strawberries. Slice them to give a good jam texture. I am using accent beads in clear purple to make blackberry jam. After the jams have been setting for a while and the resin is a lot thicker, go in with a cocktail stick or a pin and reposition the fruit, as it tends to sink to the bottom of the jar.

Making base colours for jams and jellies using resin coloured with a scrape of pastel.

Choosing the flavours of your jams and jellies.

Making jar covers

To make lids for the little jam jars I am using tissue paper, decorated with a gingham pattern using permanent marker. I have gone for blue shades, but red looks really good too. Use a ruler to make sure that the lines are straight and neat. To top the jars once the resin is fully set, use a white square overlaid with a patterned square of tissue tied round with a piece of strong button thread. This part is quite tricky and I never seem to have enough hands, so you may want to temporarily stabilise the jar with a small piece of sticky tack. Using tissue paper for the covers gives a fabric look without appearing too heavy, as real fabric could do.

Making gingham-patterned jar covers using tissue paper and thin marker pens.

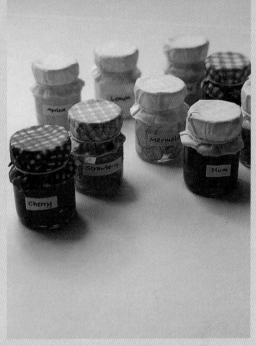

A whole rainbow of jars looks amazing displayed on the shelves of a dolls' house kitchen, larder or shop display.

Jam on toast

To create a pile of jam for toast or just as a spill on the table it is easier to use liquid clay.

Step 1: Add some pastel colour to the liquid clay and mix well.

Step 2: Mix a little translucent clay with the same colour and mash it into the liquid clay. You want this to look rough, so don't mix it too well.

Step 3: Add the fruit of your choice and arrange the mix on your baking tile in a satisfying splodge. You can also bake it straight on to the toast (*see* Chapter 2) if you want it to dribble over the edge. If you are doing this, don't forget to add a bit of butter.

Piling sticky glossy jam on toast. Lots of varnish makes this piece look extra juicy.

CHILLIES, STUFFED OLIVES AND GHERKINS

Using a similar technique to the jams, you can make all kinds of pickles and bottled foods for your shelves. The jars I've used for these are a bit bigger and tend to be stronger as well. The resin mix is just the same.

Chillies

Step 1: To make chillies, create a strip using red clay, or green for green chillies, with a piece of green clay on the top pulled out to form a ribbon of two colours.

Step 2: Cut slices of this ribbon – the size is up to you as chillies come in all sizes, just as long as they fit in the jar. Roll the slices between your finger and thumb to round them off and create a pointy end and a stalk.

Step 3: Texture the chillies by making indentations with a ball-ended tool and bake them. Arrange them in your jar of resin and allow to set.

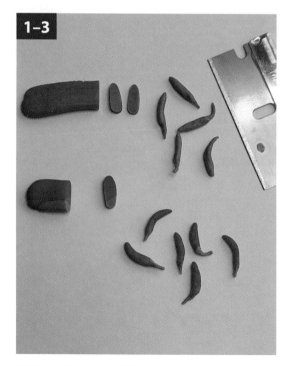

Creating red and green chillies in various sizes.

Stuffed olives

These olives look great in their preserving jar. They also look good with a slice of lemon, chilli or bay leaf added to the jar.

Step 1: Using a nice olive green and a bright red clay, create a baton of red then wrap it with a thick layer of the green. Roll this cane on the work surface to create a long cane about the width of a barbecue stick.

Step 2: Cut off some small slices of the cane and roll between finger and thumb to make them olive-shaped; try to get the red part at the pointed end of the olive. Bake these ready to add to the jar. I have also made some basic black and brown olives – all three types of olive can be combined with a few herbs and lemon pieces in the jar to make a Mediterranean olive mix.

1–2

Using a simple cane of red surrounded with green clay to make tiny stuffed olives.

Gherkins

Delicious! Absolutely my favourite and you can't have a pickle section without them. As well as looking good in a jar, these are also great on a cheese board or with a burger.

Step 1: The mix of clay for these is mostly translucent with a tiny amount of white, olive green and yellow, as most of the colour will be added later. Create tiny sausages of clay to the size you would like your pickles, but be aware that the jar magnifies them, so smaller is better.

Step 2: Texture the pickles, first with a piece of sandpaper and then a cocktail stick to make the middle really bumpy.

Step 3: With a medium-sized soft brush, add some dark green pastel colour to the body of the pickle, leaving the ends pale. Curve the pickles slightly and bake them before adding to the resin. A few added onion and mustard seeds make them look extra tasty.

Making pickled gherkins, textured with sandpaper and tinted with a little green pastel before baking.

Lovely jars of pickles look brilliant displayed with the light shining through them. Other things that look great pickled are eggs, garden vegetables, lemons and whole fruit like pears.

Creating labels for your jars

It is possible to download and print out labels for your jars, but to create simple 'handwritten' labels for your preserves adjust the font size on your computer to six or smaller if your printer is able to cope. Type the labels, leaving lots of space in between, print on thin paper and use to label the jars.

CHAPTER 11

Old English Sweet Shop

· ·

This project reminds me of old-fashioned sweet shops, with their walls lined with shelves and rows and rows of jars full of colourful treats. Memories of shiny boiled sweets like jewels, toffees in sparkly packaging and buying a little selection in a pink and white stripy bag.

Sweets and candy are great fun to create in miniature and can be used for a lot of projects, for example a bag of sweets in a child's room, to decorate a birthday cake or at the seaside or cinema. I have chosen a few old classics to make, but once you have the techniques, they can be altered to make all kinds of treats. For sizing use a scale fork; your sweets should be about the width of the prongs of the fork.

Lots of tall glass jars look great to display the colourful candies on the shelves of your dolls' house or a sweet shop.

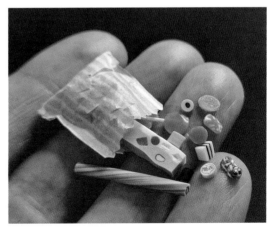

Vintage sweets are lovely to make and bring a little bit of nostalgia for childhood.

SEASIDE ROCK

A classic of the British seaside holiday, a stick of rock is a hard-boiled candy made in real life the same way as in miniature, only a lot bigger and stickier. It is made using the caning method, but because we are putting words inside we have to be quite slow and careful in order to make sure that the words stay in place when the cane is pulled.

Step 1: Knead some pieces of black and white clay in your hands to warm them up, then pull the black clay into a thick ribbon. Create the words you wish to use with the ribbon clay. Keep the words short and simple so that they are legible when shrunk down in size.

Step 2: Use shapes of white clay to hold the letters in place; an eye shape in the centre helps to create a good round shape as the cane is pulled.

Step 3: Apply even pressure around the disc of clay, checking that you have filled all gaps and the words are maintaining their shape. Continue the pressure while rotating the cane; it will start slowly to get smaller but longer to form a baton.

Step 4: Once the baton is long enough to get hold of by one end, start gently stroking the sides to pull the cane out longer. Use both squeezing and drawing out of the cane until it is about twice as long as it is wide.

Step 5: To make a striped outer layer for the rock use a very thin sheet of white clay and lay on thin batons of whatever colour you wish. Displays of rock in holiday gift shops come all the colours you can imagine, sometimes with straight stripes and sometimes twisted round like a Christmas candy cane. If you want yours twisted, begin with it straight and only when the cane is at its thinnest give it a twist – this way, you are less likely to move the writing in the centre.

Step 6: Wrap this outer skin around the fat cane of rock and then carefully continue to squeeze and stretch it. As the cane becomes long and thin, cut it into sections that are easier to handle. Once you have lots of small canes, remove the rough ends, place them in rows on your tile and bake them. Cut the sticks of rock to the exact length after they are baked but still warm. Cutting them at this point means that they will keep their round shape and the lettering will remain legible.

Creating the words inside the seaside rock using ribbons of black clay.

Securing the letters with white clay to form a disc with the letters embedded in it.

Starting to form the cane of rock, making sure to keep the words intact.

4

Slowly continue compressing and stretching out the baton shape.

5

Laying coloured stripes of clay on a very thin sheet of white clay to form the rock's outer skin.

6

Continue to lengthen the cane by gentle stroking and pulling down the length of the baton, drawing it out, making it thinner and preserving the words inside.

Sticks of rock can be created in many different colours and sizes using the caning method.

LOVE HEARTS

These fruity little sweets are so satisfying to make and people can't believe that they actually have tiny words on them as well. The method used is the same as for rock, but the finished cane is rolled a little smaller and has a heart design on it.

Step 1: Choose the colours you wish to use for your cane. The sweets come in lovely pastel shades of pink, green, white and yellow. Warm the pastel colour and red clay in your hands until soft.

Step 2: Start by creating a ribbon of red, then use the ribbon to form a word. Small ones are best, such as hug, kiss, you, love and so on, as they will need a heart around them as well as some of the pastel colour.

Step 3: Fill in around the letters to keep them in place. Add a heart shape formed with a triangle of red and a ring of the pastel clay around the edge. Make the outer ring of pastel clay quite thick so as to stop the red colour showing through too much when the cane is stretched.

Step 4: Starting with even pressure pull and press the cane, which will become smaller and longer as you turn and squeeze. Begin to draw out the cane as soon as it is long enough. Again, as the cane gets too long to manage easily, cut it into manageable lengths. Bake the canes, then cut the small rounds while the canes are still warm so as to maintain the shape.

Choosing the colours you would like for your Love Heart.

Using a ribbon of red clay, create the word for the centre of the sweet.

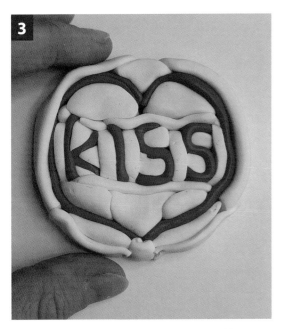

Filling the negative shapes with pastel clay and adding a heart shape and an outer ring.

Cutting the long cane into manageable lengths before baking.

In order to fill jars with these little lovelies you will need to make a few of these canes in different colours, so you may end up with a lot of sweets, but jars can make fun little gifts or even earrings or pendants.

LIQUORICE ALLSORTS

Liquorice Allsorts were definitely a favourite sweet of mine as a child. They have become a classic among miniature model-makers.

Step 1: Assemble all the colours before you start so that each type of Allsort is made with the same range of colours. Adding some translucent to each colour mix helps them to be pliable when they are layered up and not to crack apart. A little bit of white is added to each basic colour to make it a little more pastel, except for the black of course.

Step 2: The baton There are four baton-type Allsorts, which you can create using the caning method. These consist of: a basic black baton rolled as thin as a cocktail stick; a blue baton rolled thicker and on some sandpaper to give it texture (these ones are called spogs, I believe); a white baton made as a cane with a thin skin of black around it, which is rolled to toothpick width; and the most recognisable Allsort, a small baton of black with a wide band of pink or yellow around it. When pulling and rolling this last baton, leave it a little thicker; more the width of a barbecue skewer.

Make sure that all of these are nice and round and at manageable lengths, then lay them on your tile to bake. After baking, it is a good idea to cut the little sweets while the clay is still warm and easy to slice.

Step 3: The sandwich For these, use a rolling pin to create flat pieces of clay that are of equal thickness. The layers of these sometimes come apart after baking when you cut them, so to prevent this brush on a thin coat of liquid clay to stick the layers together. Pile the pieces up to create the sandwiches and then with the rolling pin flatten them to about the width of a barbecue skewer, the same size as your pink and yellow batons.

It is a good idea to put these sandwiches in the refrigerator for a while to firm up. You want your clay soft to work with, but it is better firm when cutting. Once it has chilled for a while, use the single-sided razor to cut slices into it as wide as the clay is thick. This will make cutting up the baked sweets easier and safer than trying to cut a solid slab once it has baked hard.

Step 4: The double sandwich This is basically the same as the single sandwich variety, but with two layers. These ones definitely need a layer of liquid

All the colours you need to create Liquorice Allsorts canes.

The baton Making the baton-style sweets using simple canes, one colour wrapped in another to different thicknesses.

The sandwich The layers need to be even and well stuck together in the sandwich type of sweets.

clay to keep them stuck together as they contain lots of white clay, which tends to be more brittle than other colours. Once you have rolled out these layers, they will also need chilling and cutting into lines.

Step 5: After all the components have been baked, start by slicing the sandwich-type sweets. Where you have precut lines in the unbaked clay should allow you to more easily cut or pull them apart into square batons, which can then be cut into tiny squares. Cutting while they are warm is much easier, so leave the ones waiting to be cut on the baking tile to prevent them cooling down. Now move on to the round batons, then the thin round ones, which can be cut a bit longer.

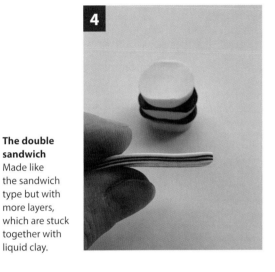

The double sandwich
Made like the sandwich type but with more layers, which are stuck together with liquid clay.

After baking the pieces, they can be cut to their final size while still warm and soft, then mixed together to create the Allsorts mix.

By changing the original colour palette – white will be the predominant colour rather than black – you can make Dolly Mixtures in the same way. Just add a few gummies made from translucent clay with a little coloured clay and textured with sandpaper.

JELLY BABIES AND WINE GUMS

Gummy sweets like jelly babies and wine gums have beautiful bright colours and a translucent squidgy appearance that is great in miniature and looks wonderful in jars or in little paper bags. The quickest way to make lots of these in different colours is to create a mould and make batches in the different colours. To make the miniature sweets we can use liquid clay, but first we need to make the mould.

Step 1: Make the blanks to create the mould. Using any colour polymer clay, create a baton of clay the thickness of a barbecue skewer and flatten it slightly so you can cut lozenge-shaped slices from it. To form these into babies make sure they are all the same height. Press in the sides to make a Russian doll shape, then cut the bottom to make legs. Then cut either side for arms and make a face using a needle. Cut either side of the baby to straighten the sides.

The blank for the wine gums is easier – just cut from a sheet of clay for the diamond shapes and slices from a baton of clay for the circles and ovals. Spend a little time getting these nice and neat and straight. I have used a cocktail stick to add some texture that looks a bit like writing to the top of the wine gums. Once you are happy with the blanks, bake them.

Step 2: Make the mould. Mix the moulding medium in equal parts, or as your brand specifies To make it a bit easier, put it into a container such as a miniature tray or a lid, then push the blanks

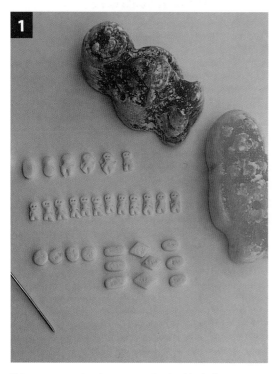

Using a razor and a pin to create the tiny blank shapes to make jelly baby and wine gum moulds.

After baking the blanks they are pressed into a silicone moulding medium to make a reusable mould.

3–4

Using liquid clay coloured with pastel to make batches of sweets in lots of different flavours. The jelly babies are dusted with a bit of talc to look powdery.

into the medium, leaving a bit of space between each one. Leave them to dry before popping the blanks out of the mould.

Step 3: Mix the liquid clay. Place a little liquid clay into a container. I often use disposable shot glasses or lids that I have saved and washed out. To colour the clay, add a scraping of coloured pastel and mix really well. Using a cocktail stick, put a little blob of the clay into each mould, wipe off the excess with a tissue and bake. Using the same method, make a batch of each colour.

Step 4: Once the sweets are baked and all the colours mixed together, the jelly babies will need a little powder to look realistic. Put them into a bag or pot and add a pinch of talcum powder or cornstarch and mix them up well. The powder should get into the little eyes and mouth and make them easier to see.

Silica sand

This method of making blanks to form a mould is great for producing batches of any shape of sweet. To make your sweets look sugary, silica sand works well and won't melt. Silica sand can be found where you buy sand and pebbles for fish tanks.

PINK AND WHITE NOUGAT

Sweets and candy are a good way to use leftover bits and bobs of clay and nougat is perfect for this. As a child I loved this pink and white nougat in a satisfying chewy slab with nuts, candied fruit and a sheet of rice paper on the bottom. For this project, I have used some leftover baked cherries (*see* Chapter 13), some translucent green from making pickles and a nut cane that we will use for the patisserie section, but really whatever you have that is pre-baked and brightly coloured can be use.

Step 1: Take some pink clay and slice it so that you can sandwich half the leftover pieces into the clay. Do the same with the white layer.

Step 2: Press down the layers together and begin to press and pull the sandwich of clay to make a brick-shaped baton that has the colours one on top of the other. Now bake the baton before cutting it into slices. The pieces inside the clay should show on the slices.

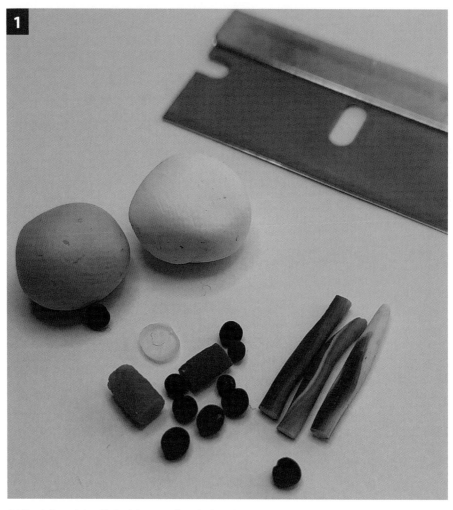

Adding leftover bits of baked clay to pink and white clay to create lovely fruity nougat.

Slicing the nougat after baking while it is still soft and warm reveals the fruity, nutty insides of the sweet, an old-fashioned fairground favourite.

CHAPTER 12

French Patisserie

. . . .

love the idea of French patisserie, all perfectly identical little desserts in jewel-coloured rows. All kinds of delicious fruits, cakes and tarts and gorgeous brown and flaky croissants. French patisserie and pastries are a lovely project to work on and look wonderful displayed in a kitchen interior, shop or café. Once the basics are made, you can work in batches and let your imagination run wild with colours, flavours and how they are arranged.

Croissants and patisserie look so elegant and delicious on your dolls' house kitchen table.

CROISSANTS

For this project we are going to make a mould so that it is possible to create lots of identical pastries, but we have to begin by making a couple of really nice croissants by hand.

Step 1: Using a pastry mix of clay consisting of white with a little caramel and golden yellow (*see* Chapter 2), form a baton that tapers to a point at each end about the width of a 1\12 dinner plate and press it slightly to flatten it a little.

Step 2: Carefully hold the centre of the baton and twist the pointed end towards you. Do this the other side, also twisting it towards you so that both sides match.

Step 3: Take a triangular flat piece of clay about half the length of the original baton and wrap this over the middle of the twisted piece. You should now have a little shape that looks a bit like a crab. At this point, you can decide if you want to make the croissants curved or straighter.

Step 4: Texture the pastry. First, press a 'V' shape in the middle of the triangle part of the croissant, then with a pin scratch some little lines into the areas where the folds are meant to be to give the impression of the layers of pastry. Bake your croissants once you are happy with them.

Step 5: I created a few croissants in this way and chose my favourite to create a mould using the silicone mould-making medium. Once you have a mould, it is much easier to start making lots of pastries. Push a small baton of clay with tapered ends into the mould, then push it out unbaked so that you can colour it. If they are too soft to pop out of the mould easily, chill them in the fridge first.

Step 6: Once you have a few pieces lined up on the baking tile, use a medium-sized soft brush to add a blush of golden-yellow pastel colour over the whole croissant, then a little burnt sienna and dark brown mix to create a baked look, starting from the base at the back and brushing over to the front. With a small fine brush add a bit of darker brown to the middle of each fold of the croissant.

Step 7: Once coloured, the croissants can be baked in the oven. Adding a bit of varnish just to the darker baked areas gives them a realistic glossy look.

Creating the croissant shape by twisting the clay and forming the sections in the pastry, then texturing them. The best croissant will be used to make a mould.

Using a mould so that you can make lots of identical pastries more easily. Colouring them gives a baked appearance.

After baking, some varnish gives the centre of each croissant a shiny baked look.

PAINS AU RAISINS AND APRICOT PASTIES

These little pastries look great in a shop display or as a breakfast item and you can easily vary the fillings with maybe raspberry jam or apple slices.

Step 1: Using the standard pastry mix, roll out thin strings of clay and wind them into spirals a little larger than the end of a pencil.

Step 2: Texture the pastry by tapping it with a toothbrush and also scratching little lines with a pin to show pastry layers. For the apricot pastry, press an indentation in the centre for the apricot to sit. Add a little dry-brushed golden-brown colour to the edges for a baked look. Next, add a little baked powder colour to the tops with a medium-sized soft brush, starting from the base towards the centre.

Step 3: Add your decorative pieces. The apricot is a little ball made from translucent clay with a tiny bit of golden yellow added. The almond slices are made with a cane created using cream-coloured clay with a really thin skin of caramel brown. This cane is pulled very long and thin, then flattened slightly to make the slices oval shaped. The cane has been baked and I have cut really thin slices and half slices to create almonds.

Creating the raisin and apricot pastries with a simple spiral of pastry-coloured clay, then texturing and colouring them.

Sprinkling almond slices on the apricot pastries.

For the raisins I have used accent beads, but just as easily you could use a very thin baton of black clay cut into tiny round slices. Try not to arrange any of the decorations too evenly on the pastries as they need to look like the pieces have been sprinkled rather than placed.

Step 4: Bake the pieces before adding icing. The reason I wait until after baking is because the liquid clay sometimes takes up the powder colour from the piece and the icing ends up a bit brown. The icing is made using liquid clay coloured with a little acrylic paint and dribbled on using a cocktail stick. To avoid any spread, let the icing sit a while on the pastries before baking, as this allows the acrylic paint to start setting, which holds the icing in place.

Step 5: Both pastries need lots of varnish after baking. Adding a cherry to the centre of a pain au raisins makes it into a Belgian bun, while a little dark brown colour rather than raisins would make a cinnamon bun. You could experiment with different-coloured additions, such as a raspberry filling or some chocolate icing.

Drizzling the icing on the pains aux raisins.

Varnishing the pastries after baking for a glossy finish.

FRENCH APPLE TART

French apple tarts are quite easy and satisfying to make and the alternative ideas are endless – pear, peach, fig, strawberry, really any flavour you like. Savoury quiches can be made the same way. First of all though, is a nice tart case. You can buy ready-made case moulds, or they can also be made using screw-top lids, toothpaste tube lids for individual cases and cupcake cases, and larger bottle caps for bigger tarts. The cases for the tarts I have made used both bought and homemade moulds and basic pastry mix. The cases are pre-baked before filling. If the top comes out a little wobbly with the

home-made moulds, you can rub the baked case on some fine sandpaper to even it up.

Step 1: To make the pastry case, you will need some pastry-mix clay rolled out thinly and cut into a circle using a cutter, icing nozzle or lid. Place this into your mould and carefully press it into the sides with a ball-ended tool. Use this tool to press a crimped pattern around the top of the tart case. Bake the case in its mould in the oven and once cool turn it out. Because it has been baked first you can't colour it with pastel, so a

Once you have decided on the size of your tart case, moulds can be made from all kinds of things; lids from tubes are particularly good.

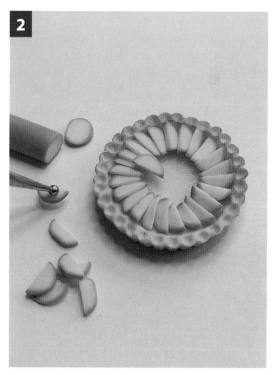

Creating a simple cane to make apple slices for your tart – judge the size of your slices against the width of the tart case.

little watered-down acrylic paint can be used to give the base and ridges on the side of the case a bit of colour.

Step 2: For the apple filling, create a baton just as you did to make whole apples (*see* Chapter 9) with a translucent centre coloured with the tiniest bit of green, yellow and white surrounded with a very thin skin of green or reddish green. The cane this time should be smaller, as this looks neater in the case – a little smaller than the width of a pencil. This can be sliced up unbaked and layered into the case in whatever pattern you like.

Step 3: Once in place, make a mix of translucent clay with a few scrapings of cream pastel colour and mix thoroughly. Carefully drip this over the filled tart. Make sure that everything has a layer of the liquid clay, but don't overfill the case as it will overflow while baking.

Step 4: After baking the tart, it can be left whole or cut while still warm to show the inside layers and used to serve on smaller plates.

Using liquid clay to cover the arrangement of apple slices in the tart case gives the whole tart a baked jelly-like texture and holds all the pieces in place.

The finished tart can be left whole or sliced to show the layers inside.

FRUIT TARTS

These tarts are so gorgeous and colourful and look great in a shop window display or on a cake stand, or even sliced up and served with cream. To make these beautiful tarts, we do the opposite of the previous tart by filling it first.

Step 1: To make the colourful layer of the tart really bright, make a mix of liquid clay and white acrylic paint and bake a thin layer of this in the bottom of the case to create a level and light-coloured layer. Now mix the fruity colour of your choice in liquid clay and pastel colour. Fill the cases almost to the top and bake.

Step 2: Add the fruit and berries; flowers would also be a pretty addition. Carefully add some clear liquid clay with a cocktail stick or fine brush and bake for the last time. These tarts will need lots of varnish to make them shiny and sticky-looking.

Using liquid clay coloured with pastel to fill the tart case and create a base layer for the fruit.

These tarts are all about how you arrange the fruit and the colours you choose. The finished desserts, once glossy and varnished, are little works of art.

LAYERED DESSERTS

These layered desserts are exactly what I think of when I think of French patisserie. Rows of perfect jewel-coloured cakes all glossy and displayed on black or gold slabs. Really sophisticated, but quite easy to make in miniature.

Step 1: Make a biscuit base from a few shades of brown, created by adding a little white to one piece of caramel-colour clay and yellow and white to another. Chop these together with a single-sided blade until they resemble crushed biscuit.

Step 2: Build the layers by creating sandwiches of colour, using both opaque and translucent clay. For some, I have used the biscuit base and for others just a pastry-coloured base. Between each layer, brush a little liquid clay to act as a glue and stop the layers separating. Once you have made the sandwiches, press them with a flat surface or a rolling pin to about 5mm deep and chill them in the fridge. Decide which dish, stand or slab you are going to put the finished pieces on, then use a single-sided blade to cut the sandwiches into rectangular pieces of the same size to fit. For the round dessert I used a large drinking straw as a cutter.

Step 3: Texture the pieces and begin adding the decoration. Using a cocktail stick, texture the

Using the chopping technique to create a biscuit base for the layered dessert.

The layers for the desserts are created like sandwiches which will then be cut to size.

biscuit base of the cakes. For the strawberry slice I created a flaky pastry texture by using a pin to scratch the pastry layer. The pastry can be coloured with a fine brush and a little pastel colour and slices of strawberry pressed into the sides.

Step 4: The chocolate slice is decorated with a tiny piece of gold leaf and a physalis, but a chocolate twirl or slice of orange would also have looked great. The round peach dessert is topped with a whole peach made from a ball of translucent and golden-yellow clay, a peach slice and a mint leaf.

After baking, the chocolate and peach cakes have had lots of varnish to make them glossy, while the strawberry slice has been decorated with a few dabs of acrylic paint to look like a layer of confectioners' sugar.

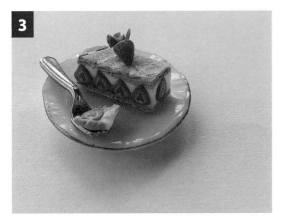

To create a flaky pastry effect on the cream slice, use a pin to scratch tiny lines along the clay and create layers to the pastry.

Using different shapes and decorations for the desserts creates a really interesting display for your French patisserie or cake shop. These are displayed on a modern-style slate board.

Making physalis

To make the physalis, use a ball tool to squash tiny slivers of caramel clay against the baking tile until they are really thin and a bit ragged, then curl up the edges, place a few of them together and add a berry made from translucent and orange clay. Bake before putting on the cake in case they collapse during baking.

Using tiny thin leaf shapes to make physalis berries to decorate the top of your layered dessert.

CHAPTER 13

Baking

• • •

BREADS

Breads are a really satisfying miniature to make. There are so many types, all linked to different cultures, festivals and times of the year. Take the time to get the texture of the fluffy or crumbly interior just right and use dry-brushing to achieve an inviting baked look. Every dolls' house kitchen needs a chopping board with a fresh loaf of bread on it to make it feel homely.

French baguettes

Baguettes are a good place to start as they are simple to make and give you a chance to practise texturing and colouring a loaf.

Step 1: Roll a few round-ended batons of white clay with a small amount of yellow and caramel brown added to form the basic pale pastry mix (*see* Chapter 2). The sizes of the real French sticks vary a lot, but as a guide a long one is about the length of two 1/12 dinner plates.

Step 2: Add leaf-shaped splits along the length of the loaf using a single-sided razor. With a toothbrush dab on some texture all over the loaf and with a toothpick draw up the clay in each split towards the middle to create a mound, as if the bread in the centre is rising out of the loaf. Dig in at the edges of the splits to define them.

Step 3: Once you are happy with the texture of the loaf, add the baked colour. Using the baked colour combination of golden yellow, warm brown and dark brown and a medium-sized soft brush, dust the colours all over to get a combination of the three. Start by brushing along the base of the loaf, working up to the top. Bread is baked from underneath, so this is the darkest area. Brush across the top rather than down from above, so that you catch and highlight the edges of the splits in the bread. You can go back with a fine brush to add any further details along the edge of the splits.

Step 4: After baking, allow the loaves to cool, then add some varnish along the flatter areas of the loaf, but not in the splits as the bread here would be dry and fluffy rather than shiny.

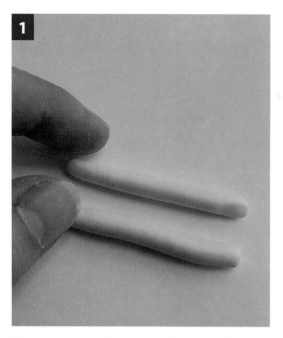

Using a basic pale pastry mix to form the simple baton shapes of French baguettes.

Texturing the bread.

Dry-brushing golden-brown colours to the base and cut edges of the loaves gives them an oven-baked look.

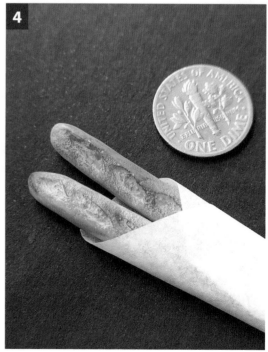

After baking, the baguettes can be given a little varnish and wrapped in paper ready for shoppers to take home for breakfast.

White sourdough

Making sourdough loaves can become a bit of an obsession. I find it is always the thing I make just for fun because there are so many ways to decorate a loaf. You can choose from a basic single split to an artisan bakery-style pattern. As ever, I suggest working from a picture of real bread, so choose a design you like and try out a few.

Step 1: Begin with a ball of very pale pastry-mix clay, as you want the inside of the bread to be creamy white. The ball should be a bit smaller than a plate so that it will fit nicely on whatever board or plate you serve it on. Cut an eye-shaped split in the top of the loaf.

Step 2: Then, just as we did with the baguette, use a toothpick to draw up from the edges of the split to the centre to make it look as if the dough has risen and burst through the crust. Make the edges of the split a little lifted and ragged. Dab texture all over with a toothbrush. If you are going to cut the loaf, now is the time to do it. If you wait until after you have coloured the piece it is much more likely that you will dab brown colour from your fingers on to the white interior of the loaf.

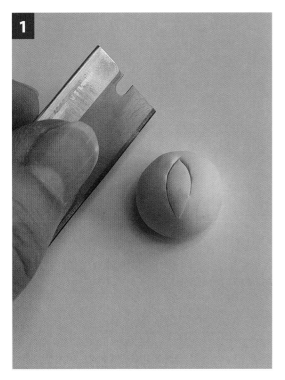

Forming a ball of dough in a rounded shape with a flat base, then slitting the top with a single-sided razor.

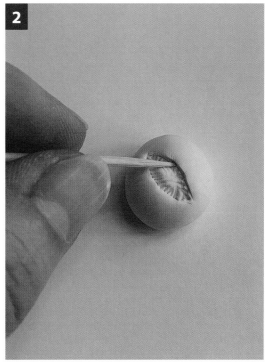

Pulling up slightly at the edges of the split, as if it has risen open.

Step 3: Use your soft brush and baked colour pastel mix to add a lovely toasty brown crust. Work from the base up, then add a little more colour along the edges of the split where the crust has browned in the oven. A fine brush can be used with a little of the darker colour to accent the edges of the split. If you are worried about getting colour on to the inside of the loaf, put a little piece of paper on the cut surface to protect it.
Step 4: Now it is time to texture the inside. Sourdough has a different crumb structure to other types of bread, so it is a good idea to have a reference picture. Using a toothpick and the finest ball tool, create tiny dents and bubbles in the bread, with the largest holes in the centre and each hole stretched a little into a semicircle. This texturing takes a while, but the tinier the dents, the better.
Step 5: When you are happy with the texture, bake the piece and then varnish just the crust areas. So as not to cover any texture on the crust, dab off excess varnish with a tissue or finger. At this point, you can also use a small brush and some acrylic paint to dab on and make a floury surface to your bread if you would like.

Colouring the bread after slicing the loaf, then texturing the inside.

After baking, the loaf can be varnished or dabbed with a little acrylic white paint to create a floury look to the top.

Wholemeal loaf

This bread is a basic brown sandwich loaf with a dry, crumbly texture. You can use the same technique to create a round shape for a rustic farmhouse loaf. This project is great for using up leftover bits of pre-mixed brown and cream clay.

Step 1: To create the wholemeal colour, use a selection of different shades of brown: caramel brown; caramel and white; caramel, white and yellow; and dark brown and white. Chop the colours together. For a wholemeal bread mix, you must keep chopping the colours until they are really fine, so that the clay at the end has a subtle and uniform pattern of colour running through it.

Step 2: Form the loaf tin shape. This is a tall rectangle that is slightly narrower at the base with straight sides, but a slightly rounded top as if the loaf has risen during baking. To make the sides and ends flat, press them against the work surface. If you are going to cut the bread, it is advisable to chill it in the fridge for a while so that you get a nice sharp edge to the slices.

Step 3: Use a toothbrush to texture the loaf all over. In this bread, the crumb is small and even, so sandpaper is also good for a texture like this. Once this is done, add a little more texture with your toothpick to the inside of the bread to make it look really crumbly.

Step 4: Use a medium-sized soft brush and the baked colour pastel mix to brush on some colour. Start from the base, then add colour along the corners and edges of the bread and a little more down the central line of the top of the loaf.

Chopping the mix of brown shades together to create a crumbly wholemeal bread mix.

Forming a rectangular loaf tin shape, then cutting slices if desired.

Texturing the loaf with a toothbrush and sandpaper after cutting any slices; a little golden-brown pastel gives the top and base a baked look.

Once baked, the finished loaf looks great on a rustic breadboard or cheese board, or sliced up ready for toast.

CAKES

Cakes are a lovely addition to a dolls' house and the variety and decoration are endless. Whether or not to cut the cakes is also a decision to be made. Cutting may spoilt your planned decoration, but on the other hand sometimes the inside of the cake is the best part and having a few slices to serve on tiny plates is a bonus.

Carrot cake

This cake is made using the same technique as the wholemeal loaf, but not chopped as finely.

By using a darker range of browns and black, you can use this method to make fruit cake or Christmas cake.

Step 1: Mix the clays to create the cake mix. I have used: caramel; caramel and white; caramel, yellow and white; and a dark orange. Begin chopping, reassemble the pieces and chop again until you have a texture that looks like carrot cake.

Step 2: Create circles of the mixture by pressing a layer of clay, then cutting out circles with a cutter, lid or piping nozzle. The circles must be smaller

Using the chopping method to create the mottled interior of the carrot cake.

Using a cutter, make even layers of the cake mix and white discs for icing, then assemble the cake.

than the finished cake, because it will all squash down thinner and wider as you assemble it. Circles the same diameter of white clay are layered between and on the top, The whole thing is now pressed together and rolled carefully along the work surface to make the sides straight. If at this point the cake is too wide, cut it to size with a cutter – it must fit nicely on your serving plate. Roll a thin layer of white around the cake. Chill the cake in the fridge for a while before cutting it.

Step 3: Cut a slice out of your cake, then using the toothpick carefully texture the cake layers; don't forget to texture the slice as well. It is easier to do this on your baking tile, so that you don't then pick up the cake and spoil the texture. Now bake the cake.

Step 4: To ice this cake, we need something that looks like a cream-cheese frosting. Acrylic texture gel mixed with white acrylic paint is perfect. Use a lolly stick or toothpick to create a texture that looks as if it has been spread with a knife on the surface. I have made some teeny carrots to decorate the cake, but orange sprinkles or orange slices would also work.

After cutting a slice from the carrot cake, texture the cake layers with a toothpick to give them a crumbly look.

A mixture of texture gel and acrylic paint can be laid on the cake after baking to make a rough, natural-looking layer of frosting.

Lemon drizzle loaf

A lemon drizzle loaf is a lovely cake to make in real life and in miniature, perfect for a simple afternoon tea.

Step 1: Using a pastry mix with a little more yellow in it, create a rectangular loaf shape a bit flatter than for the bread loaf. Again, use a photo to help with the shape. Using the single-edged razor, create a split in the top of the loaf.

Step 2: Texture the split in the loaf with a toothpick to draw up the edges into the centre where the cake has risen through the split. Use a toothbrush and toothpick to add an even texture to the outside. Slice a piece off the loaf if you wish and texture the inside in the same way, but with more of a crumbly feel.

Step 3: Add the baked colour pastel mix using a medium-sized soft brush. Use a blush of golden yellow first, then brush over with the browns. Concentrate on the base and then the edges of the cake, finishing with a little on the edges of the split at the top. Now bake the cake.

Step 4: You can now varnish the cake, adding some silica sand for sugar and some fruit, or ice it with a watery drizzle. If icing, the cake will need to be baked again. The reason I bake the cake first is that otherwise the powder colour may transfer into the icing and we don't want brown icing. Mix the liquid clay with a little bit of white acrylic paint to create a water-icing effect. Dribble the icing over the loaf with a toothpick, then re-bake. Varnish just the icing on this cake. You can add a few lemon slices, or tiny black pieces for poppy seeds or green for thyme leaves, before presenting the cake on an oval or rectangular plate.

After creating a crack along the top of the loaf, texture the sides and interior with a toothbrush.

Adding a little golden baked colour.

Icing the cake with some liquid clay and a little colour to look like watery lemon icing, before re-baking.

Black Forest gateau

This cake won't be cut, so all our energy can be spent on its outside decoration. A Black Forest gateau looks very grand as a dinner party centrepiece, or on the counter of a cake shop.

Step 1: Make a simple round shape from white clay for the body of the cake. Check the size, as we will be adding lots of layers to the outside and don't want it to get too big.

Step 2: The cherry topping consists of liquid clay mixed with a few scrapes of dark red pastel colour to create a glossy gel top for the cake. The cherries are made using translucent and a little burgundy clay mixed and rolled into tiny balls. Place the balls all over the top of the cake and cover with the gel mix. Bake the cake before beginning the next part.

Step 3: For the chocolate shards, shave off little curls of dark brown clay with the single-sided razor. Holding the cake top and bottom, dab on a little liquid clay to the sides as glue and place on the chocolate pieces with a toothpick. Try to keep them going in the same direction, but they don't have to be too neat. Once attached, the cake is baked again. This technique with the chocolate curls can be used on a chocolate Swiss roll to make an effective yule log with a little sprinkle of chalky snow.

Step 4: The icing cream consists of the no-bake acrylic gel icing. Mix some acrylic gel with a little acrylic paint really well in a pot, then place it in a small plastic bag. Seal the top of the bag and cut a tiny piece off the corner. Squeeze down the gel to the corner of the bag and use like a piping bag to add soft blobs of cream to the top of the cake. Finish the cake with some pre-baked cherries, giving them button thread for stalks. If you have any of this icing left over, it will keep for a few days without setting in the plasticine bag to use on other projects. Once everything is set, the top of this cake needs lots of varnish to make it really glossy.

After making the basic cake, cover it with cherries and liquid clay layer.

Painting on a layer of liquid clay to serve as glue helps the strands of chocolate to stick to the sides of the gateau.

After the cake is baked, use a mix of texture gel and white acrylic paint to pipe on peaks of cream.

The finished cakes are ready for a baker's window display or a charming little tea shop. Changing the colours used in the cakes gives you endless possibilities, and a few candles make it a celebration cake.

Chocolate chip cookies

This is a good project to make with leftover clay, as even one or two cookies look great resting on the side of a teacup and saucer.

Step 1: Using a drinking straw as a cookie cutter and a batch of standard pastry-mix clay, cut out a batch of circles. Use sandpaper or a toothbrush to texture the cookies and add a few bigger dents with a toothpick. Brush a little powder colour around the edges of the cookies to make them look baked.

Step 2: Using a tiny baton of dark brown clay slice off tiny pieces and place them randomly on the cookies, pressing them in a little with a toothpick. Bake the cookies, or store them in a little plastic bag until you have more things to bake.

Chocolate chip cookies are all about the texturing and dry-brushed colour that you add to make them look realistic.

You can add nuts, fruit or sweets to these cookies, but however you make them they look great displayed on a plate just waiting for a glass of milk to go with them.

Drinking straws

Drinking straws of different sizes make great cookie and pastry cutters for your tiny projects. They can even be bent to form oval or heart-shaped cutters to make identical-sized biscuits and cookies for a celebration.

CHAPTER 14

Cheese Board

· · · · · · · · · · · ·

Cheese is a great project to start, but a hard one to finish. There are so many varieties of cheese, from waxy Swiss varieties to crumbly Stilton, artisan goat's cheese and basic burger slices. Once you have begun a cheese project, you have the choice to create whole wheels of cheese for a cheese shop or restaurant, or making small slices and using them for cheese boards and platters. By adding fruit, vegetables, pickles and bread, you can make a rustic ploughman's lunch or a sophisticated after-dinner cheese board. Basic cheeses are pretty simple – it's all about the finishing touches that make them shine.

Cheese boards are such a satisfying make and there are so many things you can add to bring them to life.

SMOKED CHEDDAR

The warm golden-brown colour of this cheese looks good next to a pale cheese in a selection. As always, it is best to work from a reference photo to get the best colour mix.

Step 1: The basic cheese colour mix contains a lot of translucent clay with about one-third white, a little yellow and caramel brown. Form the mixed clay into a round cheese shape, pressed down to make it flatter on the top.

Step 2: Add the smoked colour. Unlike baked goods, the golden-brown colour is mostly in the centre of the top and sides of the cheese, rather than at the edges. For a clean slice to be removed from the cheese, it is a good idea to chill the ball in the fridge first. After it has hardened up, cut out the slices you need and bake the pieces.

Creating a basic waxy cheese mix using translucent clay with shades of yellow and caramel, all pressed into a flattened ball shape.

Cutting the cheese into wedges after dry-brushing with a rich golden brown to give a smoked appearance.

CAMEMBERT

This is a nice cheese for a selection board. Also, by changing the size and colour slightly, it can be made into brie, soft blue or goat's cheese. Camembert has two different textures – the centre uses a lot of translucent clay with a little yellow and caramel, whereas the outside is pure white clay.

Step 1: Mix the middle colour for the cheese, then roll the white clay flat and wrap it around to make a cane. You will need some extra white clay rolled to the same thickness pressed into discs.

Step 2: Take slices of the cane then two slices of white for the top and bottom. Use the warmth of your fingers to rub away the joins in the clay and form into a good camembert shape.

Step 3: Texturing the clay is important. Use a pin to press lines into the top, then make an indentation with your finger so that the cheese looks as if it has sunk a little in the middle. A small piece of tin foil that has been scrumpled up a few times to make it really wrinkly creates a great texture for the sides of the cheese.

You may choose at this point to cut a slice to expose the creamy interior of the cheese. To make the cheese look oozy, mix a little of the interior colour clay with some liquid clay and dab some of this on the inside of the cheese and the slice.

Step 4: Add some colour to the cheese. Using a medium-sized soft brush, add a little cream-coloured pastel powder brushed up from underneath and a little on the top rim of the cheese. With a little brush, highlight lightly the edges of the ridges on the top of the cheese to give a slightly aged look.

The camembert is made using a cane with a white skin that is cut into circles and finished both sides with a white layer.

Creating an oozy texture for the inside of the cheese and slice.

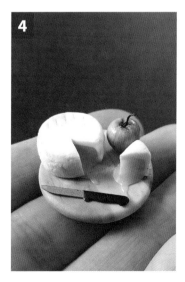

The edges of the cheese can be coloured very lightly to give a slightly aged look to the finished piece.

STILTON

Stilton is a delicious cheese that makes a statement piece for your dolls' house. It is perfect for the centre of a Victorian Christmas feast surrounded by figs, grapes and holly. Stilton slices look great on a cheese board as they provide a contrast to the yellow cheese.

Step 1: To make a wheel of Stilton, we start by making a cane. The colours of clay are: white with just the tiniest bit of yellow and caramel to create an off-white colour; white with a little more caramel for the crust of the cheese; and a combination of blue with a touch of green and dark brown mixed in to create a dark teal for the mould.

Step 2: Take half of the white and blue mixes and chop them together until there is an even amount of blue speckles in the white.

Step 3: Wrap this chopped mix in the rest of the white, then a skin of the darker cream colour. This

The colours of clay needed for the Stilton cane with its traditional blueish-green veins and creamy skin.

Taking half of the interior cheese clay, chop in the blueish-green vein colour so that it runs randomly through the mix.

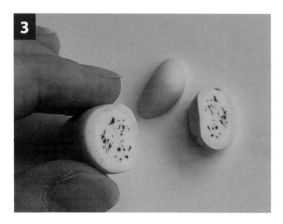

Creating a Stilton cane of mottled blue and white with a cream skin.

Pieces of Stilton ready to be textured with sandpaper and coloured.

cane is now the basis of the Stilton and can be rolled to the thickness required and cut to length. Obviously, the blue streaks will be different in every slice, so make a few and choose the ones you like best.

Step 4: After cutting the basic shapes, use some sandpaper to texture the skin of the cheese and with a toothpick add some larger holes here and there to look like the rind of a real Stilton. To texture the surfaces of the slices, press a toothpick held at an angle into the blue areas, following their natural shape. In a blue cheese, the blue mould is always slightly indented.

Step 5: Use pastel to colour the rind – a wheel of stilton looks good with a mouldy mottled exterior. Using a medium-sized brush with a flat end, first dab a little dark brown on to the surface, then light green and cream. Apply the colour randomly as it occurs naturally.

Step 6: Bake your Stilton in the oven and when baked use the same brush to apply dabs of white acrylic paint to create a powdery mould.

Adding a little white acrylic paint to the baked piece gives an extra mouldy look to the skin.

EMMENTAL

Emmental is another waxy yellow cheese, but this time with lots of bubbles running through it. It can be a wheel or semicircle, but also looks great as slices on a board, or in an open sandwich.

Step 1: The colour mix for this cheese consists of lots of translucent clay, one quarter white and a little caramel and yellow – more yellow than brown this time. Form the clay into a ball and flatten the top to create a good cheese shape. A ¹⁄₁₂ dinner plate is a good size for a wheel of cheese.

Step 2: Chill the ball before cutting. To make slices with holes, it is best to form some of the clay into a rectangular block with a rounded end. Cut your cheese wheel in half and using a small round-ended tool poke holes of various sizes, starting in the middle of the cheese and getting fewer towards the edge. Do the same to the rectangle, making sure that the holes go right through, as you will be slicing it later.

Step 3: Add a little yellow colour as a blush across the surface of the cheese and the curved end of the rectangular block.

Step 4: Bake the cheese. While the cheese is still warm, use the single-sided razor to slice a thin layer off the surface of the holey side and cut the rectangle through sideways to make slices. Be very careful doing this – the clay must be cool enough to handle, but still soft enough to cut, and take great care with the razor to keep fingers out of the way. If you are worried about doing this, you can instead chill the unbaked cheese right down and cut the slices before baking.

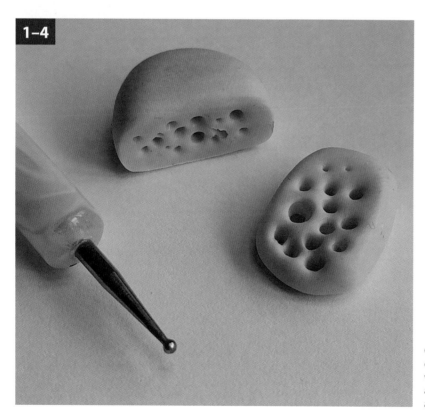

1–4

Creating, texturing and colouring a light-coloured waxy cheese mix to form an Emmental semicircle and slice.

CELERY

This is a perfect vegetable to serve with the cheese selection. It looks good left long with leaves, but also cut into little crescents in a salad.

Step 1: The mix of clay consists of translucent with white, green and a little lemon yellow. Roll the clay flat and with a bolt roll across the surface to create a set of sharp straight lines. Make sure that the bolt has rings of metal, rather than a screw with spirals that will leave diagonal lines with gaps.

Step 2: Cut along the lines to make strips of clay with vertical lines. Take some of these and wrap them round a piece of wire or a jewellery finding. Carefully pull these pieces at one end to create a thinner point but with lines still in place.

Step 3: Cut the thin end of the celery to make branches and with a ball-ended tool add some tiny rolls of clay to make more branches. Cut some tiny circles of clay and with a ball-ended tool press them against your finger to make tiny, slightly ragged leaves. Carefully add these to the stalks of celery. Before baking, give each celery stick a gentle pull to straighten it.

Be aware that putting the clay on a wire increases the temperature during baking and can cause it to burn, so keep checking the stalks for discolouration and take them out a little early. The quicker you remove the wire, the better, as it stops the baking process. This project is a little tricky, but very satisfying when you get it right and the celery is useful for lots of different projects.

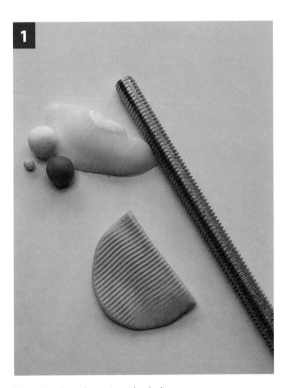

Texturing the celery mix with a bolt.

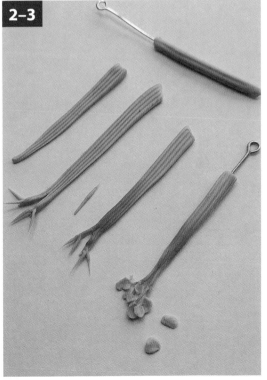

Forming various thicknesses of celery and decorating the stalks.

The celery gives a fresh pop of green colour to a cheese board and can be used for all kinds of salads.

Boards and slates

Of course, it's possible to buy boards and slabs for your cheese, but it's really quite easy to make your own. For the wooden boards, I used small wood slices from the craft store, or a rectangle cut from model-maker's wood. To cut the shape, I first drew it out to the size I wanted, then used a hacksaw to cut the rectangle, before rounding off the edges with sandpaper. Wood pieces can also be stained with acrylic paint and varnished.

Slates and marble slabs can be made using polymer clays. It is possible to get clay with a gritty granite texture, or it can be made by taking a few shades of grey clay and mixing them together to create a marbled finish. Using a plate as a size guide, roll out the clay and use a cutter or lid to cut the circles. Any rough edges can be sanded off after the boards have been baked.

Boards, slabs and slates made from clay or tiny circles cut from wood are all great to display items you have made.

CHAPTER 15

Fish

• •

Creating miniature fish is one of my favourite things. It really is all about using dry-brushing to create natural-looking colour and the simplest marks can be very effective. As always, I would suggest you work from an image of the real fish you want to create, studying its skin colours and patterns. Other useful things for this project are a piece of net fabric to create a scale pattern on the skin and some kind of shimmer powder. I have used cake shimmer, but you could use powder highlighter or craft shimmer dust. Eye shadow works too, but may contain pigments under the shimmer that will colour the clay.

Once you have mastered making fish, you can use them in lots of different dolls' house projects. You could scale down to make goldfish or fishing trophies displayed on the wall. Scale can be a bit challenging, but if you compare the fish you are making to an object such as a plate or chopping board that you have in dolls' house scale, it is easier to get an idea of how long each variety of fish should be.

All of the fish in this section begin with a clay mix of two parts white to one part translucent clay, well mixed.

A light supper dish of salmon steaks with new potatoes and asparagus.

MACKEREL

Although these fish are quite small, they have good, strong colouring and a simple shape, so I find they look effective on a kitchen table wrapped in paper.

Step 1: Working from a reference photo and using the clay fish mix above, create a simple long, narrow fish shape with a pointed face. Use a miniature plate to help you to decide the scale. Work the tail end into a point, then cut the point in half and use a ball-ended tool to open it up. You now have two leaf-shaped pieces forming the tail. Flatten these, then use a razor blade to cut a sharp point each side, creating the 'V' shape of the mackerel's tail.

Step 2: Texture the fish by using the piece of net fabric to press on a scale effect. Cut small pieces of clay to form fins in the side of the fish. Cut a slit for the gills and use the ball-ended tool to create eye sockets. Use this tool to mark the ridges down the mackerel's back and add textured lines to the fin and tail.

Step 3: Start to colour the mackerels by dry-brushing. Using a fine soft brush and your coloured pastels, start with the lighter, brighter colours – pink around the gills, a yellow eye and a yellow stripe along the centre of the body. The stripes are a dark greenish-blue and I find it easiest to apply these with a thin straight-sided brush.

The last colour to add is the black. With the same thin brush, add stripes in black between the green stripes and along the top of the fish. The face of the fish around its eyes and mouth are also black, as are its fins and tail. There is also a little black on the midline of the fish. The addition of the black really brings the fish to life.

Step 4: At this point, you can add a very gentle dusting of shimmer to the fish with a medium-sized soft brush, but be sparing.

Step 5: Add the eyes. Using either a black accent bead or a tiny ball of black clay, place this in the dents made for the eyes, then use a cocktail stick to add a tiny blob of liquid clay, which, once baked, will give you shiny, bulbous fish eyes.

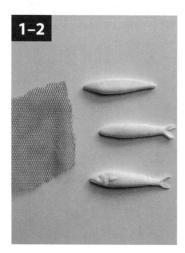

Creating the basic shape and texture of the mackerel with pointed face and a sharp tail.

Colouring the mackerels and creating stripes using dry-brushing.

Adding the finishing touches before wrapping for the kitchen table.

SEA TROUT

This is a nice big fish, so much less fiddly than mackerel to make and would be a good one for a fishing trophy or to add to a fishmonger's tray.

Step 1: This fish is longer than the mackerel and has a cut for the mouth. Using the clay fish mix (*see* above), create a basic long fish shape. Cut pieces of clay with your razor to create a dorsal fin and smaller fins by the tail. The tail of this fish is shovel-shaped – form the end of the fish to a straight edge and flatten it with your finger to make a ridge where the tail fin begins. The tail is now a spoon shape, so with the razor cut a 'V' from the centre of the tail and cut the rounded end flat.

Step 2: Create a little texture with your netting material. Cut the gills, then poke dents with the ball-ended tool for the eye sockets. Adding a few lines down the tail and fins with the ball-ended tool gives a slightly thin and ragged appearance.

Step 3: The colour on this fish is made with a little yellow ochre around the mouth, eyes and fins, plus a little red in the gills. Using the medium-sized soft brush, apply black pastel to the top of the fish. With a fine brush, add more black to the fins and tail. To create the spotty effect, wet a small fine brush and rub it on the black pastel – this will create a watercolour that you can use to add tiny spots. If the colour on the spots is too strong, after a few minutes the paint will have dried back to powder and you can soften it a little with a dry brush.

Step 4: This fish has a slight silver sheen, which can be created using cake shimmer. Add accent beads and a drop of liquid clay for the eyes. Bake the fish as you would normally and give it a shiny coat of varnish.

The sea trout is a larger fish with a dark shade across its back. The eye is added using an accent bead covered in a drop of liquid clay.

The sea trout's sheen of silver gives it a really fresh appearance. It looks great in a fishmonger's display window or in a delivery box.

PLAICE

Flat fish like plaice make a nice addition to a fishmonger's stall as they are so different to other kinds of sea food.

Step 1: Plaice vary in size, but generally are about the size of a side plate. Using the basic fish clay mix (*see* above), make a diamond shape with a slightly longer tail end. With your finger, squash down the end of the tail to make a spoon shape, then cut it straight at the end. Using the ball-ended tool, decide where the body shape of the fish will be, then draw out the wings from that shape to create an outer frill around the inner fish body. The flat fish's face is sideways on; it has one eye indent on the top and one to the side. Its face is a little pointed.

Step 2: Using your netting again, add a little texture to the body of the fish. With a razor, give the fish a gill around the eye; this is where you really need a reference photo because the poor old flat fish's face is rather strange. The wings and tail of the fish need a few lines made with the ball-ended tool to thin them out at the edges and give them a natural look.

Step 3: Colouring the fish is done in three stages. First, with a medium-sized soft brush blush around the edges of the fish with yellow ochre. The middle part of the fish is a greeny-brown mix, again just brushed on with the medium-sized soft brush. This fish has camouflage spots on its skin, so with a small, fine brush and a little water wet the paste to create a watercolour. Add some spots of a reddish-brown on the body and fins.

Step 4: After baking, apply plenty of varnish to make the plaice look shiny and wet.

Creating the diamond shape of the plaice with fins splayed out at the sides and a little squashed face.

Adding colour layer by layer gives real depth and the spots create the camouflage look of this flat fish.

The baked and varnished plaice looks great on a slab with some ice.

RED MULLET

This is a really pretty fish and a bit unusual – it gives a Mediterranean feel to a fishmonger's display. It could be scaled down to become a pond fish or even a goldfish.

Step 1: Using the basic fish clay mix (*see* above), form a slightly squat goldfish shape with a head that points downwards. Form the tail by creating a point, then cutting this down the middle. Using a ball-ended tool, splay out the tail and shape it.

Step 2: Texture the fish by pressing with the netting fabric. Add the fins and create lines in them with the ball-ended tool. Use the same tool to create the eyes, then the razor to cut in gills.

Step 3: Colouring this fish is the fun part, as you get to use all the beautiful sunrise colours. Using

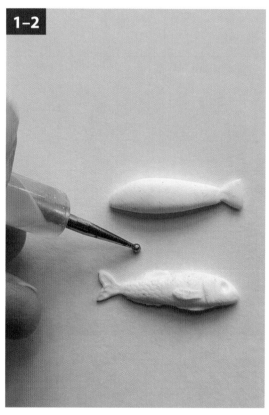

Forming the red mullet from a basic goldfish shape and adding texture with netting.

Starting with the lightest and building up lots of bright sunrise colours for this fish.

the medium-sized brush, create a midline on the fish with golden yellow; make the fin and tail yellow. Use an orangy-red along the top of the fish and around its face and fins. Using a fine brush, give the fish a strong red eye.

Step 4: For this fish I chose to use a gold shimmer powder along the back and gills, but go gently as you don't want it to end up looking like a goldfish. An accent bead or tiny ball of clay covered in a tiny blob of liquid clay brings up that shiny red eye.

Step 5: After baking, give the fish a coat of gloss varnish and decide how you would like to present it.

Adding a little gold lustre dust and eyes to your red mullet.

This brightly coloured fish looks beautiful served on a white 'marble' slab, but would also be great on a barbecue.

Ice

Making the ice for displaying your fish, meat or fruit is simple. Create a reusable mould by pressing coarse rock salt into a mould-making medium. Once set, shake out the salt and make the ice using uncoloured liquid clay baked in the mould.

GRILLED SEA BASS

Of course, you don't want all of your fish to be raw, so this is how to turn a basic fish into a crispy barbecued feast stuffed with lemon and herbs. It is a dish that is timeless and could be cooking over a medieval fire as easily as in a modern frying pan or barbecue.

Step 1: Choose the type of fish you want to cook – any type would work, from a big salmon to some little sardines all in a row, but for this project I have chosen the sea bass. Form the shape of the sea bass using the basic fish clay mix (*see* above).

Step 2: As before, use netting to create the scales. I think that a cooked fish looks good with an open mouth, so cut that as well as slashes for the gills. Also cut a slit along the belly and in the sides to stuff the fish, just as you would prepare a fish for cooking.

Step 3: The sea bass is coloured in two stages. First, start with soft colours: pink around the gills, the slit in the belly and sides; then a little golden yellow around the eye. Using the medium-sized soft brush, paint a blush of black along the top line of the fish and on the fins and tail. A gentle brush with shimmer to bring up the scales is next.

The second part is to make the fish look cooked. Using a fine brush and some dark brown, add colour to the edges of the slash marks, the fins and the tail. With a medium-sized soft brush, paint some black up from under the fish all around, as if it were being burnt from underneath. Adding a few ragged slashes to the fin tips and tail make it look as if some of it has burnt away.

Use an accent bead for the eye as usual, but adding just a scrape of white pastel to the liquid clay gives a milky look once baked, which is how cooked fish eyes appear. Tiny rolled pieces of green clay make good herbs to add to the top of the fish and to put inside for stuffing. Lemon also looks good, or maybe tomato or onion slices.

Step 4: After the sea bass has been baked, give it a coat of varnish and maybe serve it with a nice salad.

Make the body of the sea bass, but cut some slashes in the sides and along the belly so that it can be stuffed with herbs and lemon.

After dry-brushing on the basic colours, the tail and fins can be roughed up and darker browns and blacks brushed on to show the cooked areas.

The finished sea bass has a realistic baked look – great for a dinner table, or on a barbecue by the sea.

SALMON STEAK

The salmon steak is made as a cane and if kept in a plastic bag uncooked can be used for lots of projects. Because of how it is made, the cane can be used to create a whole fish or fillets, or a slice of smoked salmon – it all depends how you cut it. The whole project looks quite complicated, but if you just follow each step, it isn't too difficult and you end up with salmon for endless projects.

Step 1: The first decision to make is whether you want your salmon to look cooked or raw. Cooked salmon can be used for whole salmon, fillets and steaks, while the raw can be used for all of these plus smoked salmon and sushi. The mix of clay I have used is translucent, with white plus a little yellow, red and caramel brown. This makes a mix that looks like lightly cooked salmon.

For a raw mix, use one-third of the white and a little more of the coloured clays. It is best, however, to start with the tiniest amount of the coloured and add more, as pigments in different clays can vary a lot. Whichever you choose, make a good

Making the colour mix for the salmon fillets' flesh.

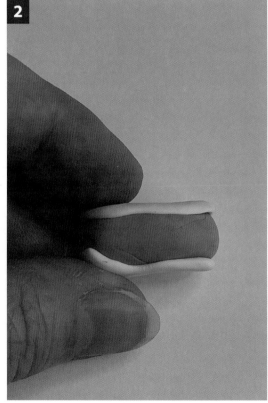

Forming sandwiches of salmon flesh to be cut into strips.

amount as it may be hard to match the colour if you don't have enough and need to make more.

Step 2: Once you have mixed a clay colour you are happy with, mix a second batch of just white with a bit of translucent to make it flexible and create a sandwich with the clays, consisting of a thick slab of salmon colour in the centre and thinner white layers either side.

Step 3: Using a rolling pin, roll out the sandwich into a large squarish shape and cut it into strips. Layer two strips and wrap them round a smaller third piece to make a semicircle.

Step 4: Add half a strip above the semicircle and four strips below of ever decreasing size. What you have now is starting to look like a piece of salmon.

Step 5: Wrap the salmon in a thin layer of white to hold it together and begin to squeeze the cane to make it smaller and longer. Work your way around the cane, squeezing gently to maintain the shape.

Step 6: Continue to compress the steak evenly on all sides so that it begins to get smaller and thicker. Once it is about twice as long as it began, cut it into two equal halves.

Step 7: The cane now needs to be made more steak-shaped. Make a baton of clay with translucent in the centre wrapped in white, which will be the bone in the centre of the steak. And two pieces of white clay, one triangular and one oval. The two sides of the steak will now fit either side of these shapes.

Step 8: Mix white, translucent and a little grey to form a skin. Wrap a thin layer of the skin around the cane, then continue to squeeze and pull, hanging the cane from your hand and running your other hand down the length of the clay to draw it down whilst maintaining the pattern inside.

Using the strips of clay to begin to form the patterns within the salmon flesh.

Add to the curls of salmon with pieces of the cut strips until you have a realistic half-salmon steak.

Wrapping the shape, then gently compressing it to begin making the cane.

Step 9: The finished cane can now be cut to whatever length you wish for steaks or whole fish.

Step 10: When making steaks, cut off a slice and use a drinking straw to cut out the oval shape at the base of the slice. Use the ball-ended tool to tease the steak into shape. Add a dent to the bone in the centre.

Step 11: To create a whole fish, use a longer piece of cane and pull it to make it narrower at one end. Net can be used to give the skin a scaly texture and a little shimmer of dark grey brushed along the top of the fish. If the fish cane is wrapped in plastic, it can be kept unbaked to use for dressed salmon, sushi, smoked salmon or a simple fish supper.

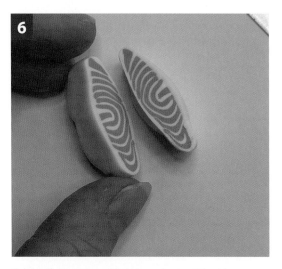

Halving the cane once it is twice as long as it is wide.

Starting to form a steak shape.

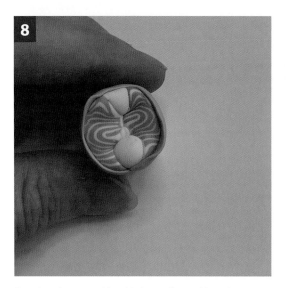

Covering the cane with a thin layer of grey skin and continuing to pull it longer.

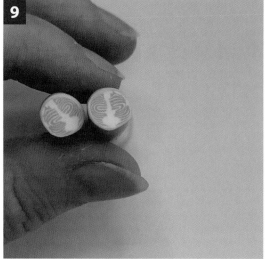

The finished cane can be cut to whatever length you wish.

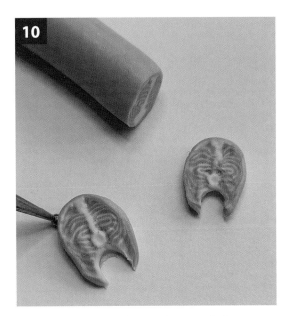

Texturing and shaping salmon steaks using a ball-ended tool.

The cane can also be used to make a whole fish.

A lovely display table piled high with baked goods.

Index

• • •

First published in 2024 by
The Crowood Press Ltd
Ramsbury, Marlborough
Wiltshire SN8 2HR

enquiries@crowood.com

www.crowood.com

British Library Cataloguing-in-Publication Data
A catalogue record for this book is available from the
British Library.

ISBN 978 0 7198 4402 7

Typeset by Envisage IT
Cover design by Sergey Tsvetkov
Printed and bound in India by Parksons Graphics Pvt. Ltd.

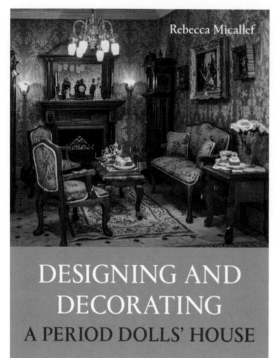

Rebecca Micallef

DESIGNING AND
DECORATING
A PERIOD DOLLS' HOUSE

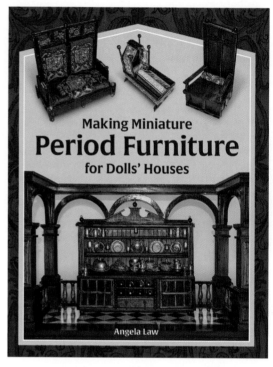

Making Miniature
Period Furniture
for Dolls' Houses

Angela Law

MAKING
MINIATURE SCENES

SHARON HARVEY

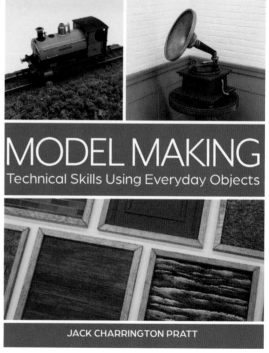

MODEL MAKING
Technical Skills Using Everyday Objects

JACK CHARRINGTON PRATT